JUST PRAY

30 Days Of Encouragement:
God's Not Done With You!

Sheila Alewine
www.aroundthecornerministries.org

Around The Corner Ministries exists to take the gospel to every neighborhood in America. Our mission is to equip followers of Jesus to engage their neighborhoods and communities with the gospel of Jesus Christ.

A WORD TO THE READER

Every one of us experiences times in our lives where we feel unqualified or ineffective in God's kingdom work. We live in a culture that glorifies physical beauty and strength, extreme skills, and dazzling talents. Life is a competition, and if we don't stand out, or have special gifts, then the world considers us mostly unremarkable and of little use.

We all struggle with moments of doubt about our usefulness to God, but never so much as when our physical bodies start to fail us. We start to grow older; we tire easily; our muscles weaken, along with our sight and hearing. Sickness, disease, or physical tragedies can steal our health at any age. Our once busy and active pace grinds to a crawl as we face the reality of things we simply cannot do. And along with those physical challenges come the emotional and spiritual battles of where we fit into the purpose and plan of God's work.

If you find yourself thinking, "What good am I to the kingdom anymore?" this devotional is for you.

We believe you are strategically and sovereignly positioned to have kingdom impact in this generation through a simple commitment to prayer. How often have you heard someone say, "All I can do is 'just pray'!" The reality is, the most powerful and effective thing we can do is pray.

What would happen if today's generation of aging saints decided to ask God for an army of laborers to be sent out into His harvest? What would happen if every believer who is limited by their physical abilities decided to focus their time and attention on seeking God's heart and pleading for God's Spirit to bring a fresh revival to our world? What would happen if we *all* joined as a unified body to pray for a great movement of the Spirit in our own communities?

God is not looking for people of strength and confidence. He is seeking those who know they are helpless and weak so that His strength and glory can be made magnified in us. No matter what challenges or limitations you may have, God still has work for you to do for the kingdom. **He's not done with you yet!**

We invite you to accept the challenge and *just pray*.

The righteous man will flourish like the palm tree,
he will grow like a cedar in Lebanon.
Planted in the house of the Lord, they will flourish in the courts of our God.
They will still yield fruit in old age; they shall be full of sap and very green,
to declare that the Lord is upright;
He is my rock, and there is no unrighteousness in Him.
Psalm 92:12-15

TABLE OF CONTENTS

A Word To The Reader   Page 3

Uniquely Gifted To Pray   Page 7
Day 1 – Day 5

A Clear Command To Pray   Page 19
Day 6 – Day 14

A Proven Pattern Of Prayer   Page 39
Day 15 – Day 20

The Power Of Prayer   Page 53
Day 21 – Day 25

A Practical Path To Prayer   Page 65
Day 26 – Day 30

A Final Word   Page 77

UNIQUELY GIFTED TO PRAY
Day 1 – Day 5

I have become a marvel to many, for You are my strong refuge.
My mouth is filled with Your praise and with Your glory all day long.
Do not cast me off in the time of old age;
do not forsake me when my strength fails.
O God, You have taught me from my youth,
and I still declare Your wondrous deeds.
And even when I am old and gray, O God, do not forsake me,
until I declare Your strength to this generation,
Your power to all who are to come.

Psalm 71:7-9,17-18

You are uniquely gifted to pray.

Your challenges, your limitations, and your fears have perfectly
positioned you to know God in an intimate way and experience His heart.
Your experience and wisdom gained from
persevering in the trials of life are precious and needed.

God is inviting you take your place in His kingdom work,
a treasured child at the table of provision and blessing.

How will you use these gifts?

Accept the challenge of a life committed to pray,
and watch God use you to impact the kingdom
beyond what you can imagine.

Day 1: The Gift Of A God-Sized Task

Take It In

Joshua 14:6-12 – *Then the sons of Judah drew near to Joshua in Gilgal, and Caleb the son of Jephunneh the Kenizzite said to him, "You know the word which the Lord spoke to Moses the man of God concerning you and me in Kadesh-barnea. I was forty years old when Moses the servant of the Lord sent me from Kadesh-barnea to spy out the land, and I brought word back to him as it was in my heart. Nevertheless my brethren who went up with me made the heart of the people melt with fear; but I followed the Lord my God fully. So Moses swore on that day, saying, 'Surely the land on which your foot has trodden will be an inheritance to you and to your children forever, because you have followed the Lord my God fully.' Now behold, the Lord has let me live, just as He spoke, these forty-five years, from the time that the Lord spoke this word to Moses, when Israel walked in the wilderness; and now behold, I am eighty-five years old today. I am still as strong today as I was in the day Moses sent me; as my strength was then, so my strength is now, for war and for going out and coming in. Now then, give me this hill country about which the Lord spoke on that day, for you heard on that day that Anakim were there, with great fortified cities; perhaps the Lord will be with me, and I will drive them out as the Lord has spoken."*

Think It Through

Here is where we begin, listening in on Caleb's conversation with his old friend Joshua. They have a lot of history together, and Caleb's request probably doesn't surprise Joshua. They have spent the last forty-five years enjoying a God-sized adventure they never planned. Perhaps they knew each other as boys, and grew up at each other's homes, teasing their siblings and getting into mischief. You would think they would both be ready to retire and settle in for a few years of inactivity and rest – a well-earned reward for a life of hard work.

Not Caleb! We see from his words that he feels as strong as ever, and he is ready to claim the promise that Moses gave him so many years ago. He asks for a mountain to climb and another God-sized task to complete.

Our twenty-first century lives have certainly improved over the last hundred years, and many people enjoy a long and healthy life. But even if we come to the last part of our lives having left behind our good health and mobility, we believe God still has purpose and a mountain for us to scale.

During the next thirty days, we'll refer to Caleb and all those who are of (somewhat) similar age, as "aged saints." I love this term, and if you fall into that category, please know that it is a term of endearment and honor.

"Aged" simply means that you've got some years behind you. Aged cheese is a fine delicacy, and aged wine is more valuable. Your experiences have given you an advantage that your younger brothers and sisters have yet to gain. It doesn't mean you're out of date or no longer useful. In fact, it means just the opposite. God has allowed you to grow in wisdom, knowledge, and experience, and He has a purpose for the years at the end of your life.

"Saints" are those very special people that God has called into His family and made His very own children. They are the ones who have had their spiritual eyes opened and believe. They are the saved, the faithful, the chosen. If you know Jesus, you're a saint!

Live It Out

The reality is, we all have a limited number of days to enjoy our lives on this earth. There's only so many hours left to spend, so we must decide how we will use them. As citizens of God's kingdom, there is much to be done, and our physical limitations and age are not hindrances, but they are divinely empowered advantages to be a part of something precious to God – the spread of the gospel for His glory.

God has ordained our days, and retirement doesn't begin until the close of our last day on earth! Will you be like Caleb and accept the challenge of a God-sized task perfectly designed for the aged saint? This is our desire for you.

Psalm 139:16 – *Your eyes have seen my unformed substance; and in Your book were all written the days that were ordained for me, when as yet there was not one of them.*

Pray Today

Dear Father, How much I want to be like Caleb! He was full of courage and spirit even at eighty-five years old. Some of us are nearing that age, or are already there, and our physical bodies do not feel like climbing a mountain. But I believe You still have a purpose for me, and work for me to do in Your kingdom. Open my eyes to what You have in front of me and help me to trust You to use me for Your glory. In Jesus' Name, Amen.

Day 2: The Gift Of Limitations

Take It In

2 Samuel 4:4 – *Now Jonathan, Saul's son, had a son crippled in his feet. He was five years old when the report of Saul and Jonathan came from Jezreel, and his nurse took him up and fled. And it happened that in her hurry to flee, he fell and became lame. And his name was Mephibosheth.*

Think It Through

If I asked you for your first memory, what would it be? Psychologists tell us about a phenomenon called "childhood amnesia" which causes us to forget the details about our lives before the age of three. While you're a child, you can remember, but as you approach age six or seven, those early memories fade.

It's God's grace that allows us to forget our earliest days, because many of us experience great trauma at a very young age, and we would never get past those events if we were able to remember them in detail. In fact, God's grace can help us overcome any physical or emotional trauma, no matter what age it happened.

Perhaps that was how it was with Mephibosheth. From birth he had known the life of a prince. He learned to walk in his grandfather Saul's palace. He watched his father, Jonathan, and the rest of his aunts and uncles enjoy a privileged life of royalty. He literally ate at the king's table, and his every need and want was indulged.

Then one night, at five years of age, he is roughly awakened from sleep by his nurse. There is chaos and noise and shouting. His nurse jerks him up from his bed and pulls him through the hallways, urging him to hurry. His father and his grandfather have been killed in battle, and the kingdom is lost. They are running for their lives, afraid that the new king will be coming to kill the rest of the family. Maybe his nurse tripped and dropped him, or she pulled him along so quickly that he couldn't keep up. We don't know exactly how, but his life changed dramatically that night and he became lame in both legs.

He lost his family. He lost his home. He lost his physical abilities. From that night on, he wouldn't even remember what it felt like to run and play. In many ways, his identity became "the boy who is lame."

Live It Out

Yesterday we talked about a group of people like Caleb, an assembly of *aged saints.* Maybe you're not like Caleb at all, but you can identify with

Mephibosheth: it's not your age that limits you, but your physical body. Perhaps it's something you were born with: a debilitating condition that keeps you from joining in when the rest of the world moves on. Possibly it's something that happened to you as a child or a teenager– an accident or a sudden illness – that stripped you of your physical ability to participate in life's opportunities.

Maybe you've been thinking that those limitations have excluded you from doing "important" kingdom work; that God can't use you like He uses other people. You've been sitting on the sidelines wondering where you fit in and what value you bring to the body of Christ.

Mephibosheth probably asked himself what value he brought to the kingdom. After all, a man with two lame feet would make a poor warrior. But listen to what his name means: *exterminating the idol*, or *dispeller of shame*. Right there in Mephibosheth's name we can find our identity as a child of God, and that identity lays the foundation for our value to the kingdom, regardless of our physical ability, mental stamina, life experiences, or age.

As a child of God, we have exterminated the idols in our lives; we have turned away from our old lives to serve the One True King, Jesus.

As a child of God, our shame has been dispelled. Our sins have been forgiven and we are counted worthy, accepted, redeemed and reconciled to God. We are co-heirs with King Jesus.

God has purpose for our lives, and it's not dependent in the least on our physical abilities, our age, or our giftedness. It's grounded deeply in our identity in Christ, as a child of God and as a child of the kingdom.

Are you a Mephibosheth?
Do you need to remember your name?

Hebrews 12:12-13 – *Therefore, strengthen the hands that are weak and the knees that are feeble, and make straight paths for your feet, so that the limb which is lame may not be put out of joint, but rather be healed.*

Pray Today

Dear Father, I may have challenges, but I know that I still have value and purpose for Your kingdom. The enemy often tells me I am useless, and that while I'm on this earth, I just need to sit on the sidelines and let Your other children do the "real" work of serving You. I know that is a lie. Help me to recognize the truth of my identity in You and discover how You want to use me for Your glory. In Jesus' Name, Amen.

DAY 3: THE GIFT OF GOD'S HEART

Take It In

Joshua 14:7-8 – *I was forty years old when Moses the servant of the Lord sent me from Kadesh-barnea to spy out the land, and I brought word back to him as it was in my heart. Nevertheless my brethren who went up with me made the heart of the people melt with fear; but I followed the Lord my God fully.*

Think It Through

If we are going to follow God fully into a great adventure, we must have His heart. This was the distinguishing feature between Caleb and Joshua, and the other ten Israelites who were sent to spy out the promised land. The report that came back exposed what was in their hearts.

Caleb was committed to following the Lord fully. He did not only think about God on the days of required sacrifice and worship, but everything he did centered on pleasing God and honoring Him with his life. God was not simply a part of his life; He *was* his life. As a result, he was confident in God's desire and ability to give them the land and brought back a good report. **He had God's heart.**

How do we get God's heart? How do we begin to see the people in our lives through the eyes of Jesus? How do we gain God's perspective of our world?

We ask Him for it.

Prayer is the key to God's heart, and specifically prayer for others. As we begin to intentionally and consistently lift our requests to Him, we begin to love those for whom we pray. God's Spirit and His Word give us direction in how and what to pray, and we soon find ourselves thinking about others in a new way.

We will grieve because others do not know the Lord.
We will hurt when others suffer.
We will rejoice when others are glad.

Caleb had God's heart because He followed the Lord fully. He pursued God with a desire to live and speak and act in ways that honored God. Just like his friend Joshua, he most likely would have spent time in the tent of meeting, praying to God for his family and his people (Exodus 33:11)

Live It Out

Caleb's heart for the Lord did not diminish with age. We are mistaken if we believe that God only uses young people or seemingly talented people in the important places of kingdom work, and that once we reach a certain age we can relax and coast into old age on our past commitments. Our roles may change, but the Holy Spirit within us is always young, and we can continue to grow in our passion for God's heart. We are still members of the body of Christ, still gifted and vital to God's kingdom purposes.

The same God who called young Caleb to spy out the land also called eighty-five-year-old Caleb to conquer a mountain named Hebron. You see, we will grow old and tired, but God is eternal, and His power never wanes. We may think it was our strength that God used in the days gone by, when we rounded up preschool children, or built homes for the needy, or preached on the streets of a third-world country. But the reality is, it was all God's power then, and you can take hold of that same power today, no matter what your physical strength may be.

Do you have God's heart?
Are you still following the Lord fully?

Then consider making prayer your Mount Hebron and take hold of God's strength and power. He has kingdom work for you to do.

Deuteronomy 13:4 – *You shall follow the Lord your God and fear Him; and you shall keep His commandments, listen to His voice, serve Him, and cling to Him.*

Pray Today

Dear Father, I want Your heart. I want to see the world around me through Your eyes. I want to feel Your compassion for my neighbors, my friends, and my family. I want to know how to pray. I may not be as strong and able as I used to be. I get tired and am easily discouraged when I feel that I'm just not useful to You anymore. But I realize that is not true, and that You have a place for me in Your kingdom purposes. Help me to remember that I'm not home yet. Give me Your strength to follow You fully, whole-heartedly, just like Caleb. In Jesus' Name, Amen.

DAY 4: THE GIFT OF THE KING'S INVITATION

Take It In

2 Samuel 9:3-7,13 – *The king [David] said, "Is there not yet anyone of the house of Saul to whom I may show the kindness of God?" And Ziba said to the king, "There is still a son of Jonathan who is crippled in both feet." So the king said to him, "Where is he?" And Ziba said to the king, "Behold, he is in the house of Machir the son of Ammiel in Lo-debar." Then King David sent and brought him from the house of Machir the son of Ammiel, from Lo-debar. Mephibosheth, the son of Jonathan the son of Saul, came to David and fell on his face and prostrated himself. And David said, "Mephibosheth." And he said, "Here is your servant!" David said to him, "Do not fear, for I will surely show kindness to you for the sake of your father Jonathan, and will restore to you all the land of your grandfather Saul; and you shall eat my table regularly." ... So Mephibosheth lived in Jerusalem, for he ate at the king's table regularly. Now he was lame in both feet.*

Think It Through

Mephibosheth's circumstances had taken him to a place he didn't belong. He was living somewhere that God had never intended but was there because the world is broken. Heartache and pain are an unavoidable part of life. Does his situation sound familiar to you?

King David was still grieving over the tragedy that had befallen Saul's family. David had God's heart, and he remembered his good friend Jonathan, and desired to honor him. So, he sought out Mephibosheth, the one who had been pushed aside and left behind, the one who had suffered greatly as God stripped the kingdom from his wicked grandfather, Saul, and passed it to his chosen servant, David.

Mephibosheth was living in the house of Machir, the son of Ammiel, in a place called Lo-debar. Machir means "sold." Ammiel means "my kinsman is God." And Lo-debar, the place where he was living in exile, means "not a pasture" or "pastureless." These names tell his story, and perhaps you can see your own narrative, for we, too, were exiles like Mephibosheth. We are **sold** as slaves into sin from birth (Romans 7:14) but our **Kinsman Redeemer, Jesus**, came to give us a new identity (Galatians 3:13, 4:5; 1 Peter 1:18) and restore us back to the family. We were exiles living under the dominion of our enemy Satan, but we have been rescued and brought into the fold, into His **pasture**. We are restored to the kingdom, invited to sit at the **King's table** (Colossians 1:13, Psalm 23).

Live It Out

Every Christ-follower has a new identity and a place at the table of God's kingdom. Our worth to the kingdom has nothing to do with our physical, mental or emotional abilities, or even our spiritual maturity. We have a place at the table because the God of the universe sent out a rescue party in the form of His Son, Jesus. This is our true worth, our God-given identity. We are restored to the family by the grace of God because God thinks we're worth the life of His Son.

Have you been feeling a bit exiled?
Have your limitations been masquerading as your true identity?
Have you felt your worth was based on what you could contribute to the cause of Christ?

Let Mephibosheth's story remind you that God has purpose for your life, and that you have a part to play in His kingdom. Your circumstances, challenges, limitations and failures all uniquely gift you to see the power of God and impact the world right where you are. If you can pray, you can move mountains. Prayer gives God the opportunity to reveal His power and glory in a way that no physical feat will ever touch.

How do you take your place at the table? Like Mephibosheth, you simply offer yourself as the King's servant and accept His offer of grace. You move into His house and come to the table. There you will find what He has already prepared for you to do.

John 10:9-10 – *I am the door; if anyone enters through Me, he will be saved, and will go in and out and find pasture. The thief comes only to steal and kill and destroy; I came that they may have life, and have it abundantly.*

Pray Today

Dear Father, What grace we see in Mephibosheth's life! Like all of us, he felt inadequate and unworthy to sit at the King's table. He felt his life was useless when compared to those with more health, more ability, more talent. But you have purpose for every one of us. When we accept your offer for a place at the table, our limitations become unique platforms for Your power to be revealed. As we dedicate our lives to prayer, we will experience You in a way that we never imagined. Help us to believe this, and to find our identity and worth only in You. In Jesus' Name, Amen.

DAY 5: THE GIFT OF COMMITMENT

Take It In

2 Timothy 4:7-8 – *I have fought the good fight, I have finished the course, I have kept the faith; in the future there is laid up for me the crown of righteousness, which the Lord, the righteous Judge, will award to me on that day; and not only to me, but also to all who have loved His appearing.*

Romans 12:12 - *...rejoicing in hope, persevering in tribulation, devoted to prayer.*

Think It Through

When Paul writes these words to his beloved child in the faith, Timothy, he is approaching the end of his life. History tells us he met Jesus on the Damascus Road in 34 AD. After 32 years of ministry, he has come to the end of his life in a damp Roman prison, knowing that he will soon face execution at the hands of Nero. Twice in this letter he urges Timothy, "Make every effort to come to me soon" (4:9, 4:21). Most of his traveling companions have either deserted him or have been sent on other missions; only his dear friend and physician, Luke, remains close by.

These are the last words of Paul contained in scripture and it is a call to perseverance and commitment. Paul warns Timothy that hard and difficult times are coming, but he must not abandon his faith. Paul has set the example in a ministry faced with persecution, affliction and rejection. He has been physically beaten, socially ostracized, doubted, questioned, and mocked. His very life has been in danger many times, yet he has remained faithful and diligent; fully committed to "being poured out as a drink offering" to the Savior he loves. And it is this same endurance that he challenges Timothy to imitate.

What is the "good fight" that Paul has fought?
What is the "course" he has finished?

It is the mission of the gospel that God called him to proclaim. God set him on this course of suffering, *a chosen instrument to bear His name before the Gentiles and kings and the sons of Israel* (Acts 9:15-16). He was given a gift – a mystery to unfold (Ephesians 3:1-13). He carried a burden for his own people, the Jews, but was sent to the Gentiles, preaching the gospel in hopes that his fellow Israelites would grow jealous and repent and receive salvation (Romans 11:11-14).

Live It Out

The Greek word used to describe Paul's fight as "good" is *kalos* and means "beautiful, honorable, fair, precious, praiseworthy and noble." Paul knew that the fight was good because of the priceless value of the gospel for which he fought. His life was difficult and every day he had to draw on the unlimited grace and power of God to sustain him. I'm sure there were many days he felt like giving up and giving in. But he persevered because he knew the eternal souls of men were at stake.

How are you persevering in your faith? Are you committed to living out your faith in the face of difficulties, fully engaged in the spiritual work that God has called you to? Or have you been listening to the enemy's suggestion that you are no longer needed in the battle?

Paul tells us that devotion to prayer goes hand-in-hand with perseverance in tribulation and is sustained by hope that rejoices (Romans 12:12). Keeping our eyes fastened on Jesus, and the glory to come, will help us persevere and fulfill our commitment to follow Christ all the days of our lives, despite the hardships of life.

Maybe you're like Paul and have fewer days ahead of you than behind you. Or you may be like Timothy, with a life of suffering, adversity, and spiritual warfare ahead. Regardless, we all need to persevere in what God has called us to do and be willing servants who will pour our lives out for the good fight, finish the course, and keep the faith. And we do this by the grace and power of God that never wavers.

Romans 15:4 - *For whatever was written in earlier times was written for our instruction, so that through perseverance and the encouragement of the Scriptures we might have hope.*

Pray Today

Dear Father, Thank you for Paul's wise words. He challenges us to set aside our own inclination to coast into heaven, letting others fight the good fight on our behalf. We know that as long as we live, we have purpose in Your kingdom; our reward is laid up in heaven for us, and we must persevere and remain faithful until You determine it's time for us to receive it. Give us grace and endurance to finish our course and remain committed and faithful until we see You face to face. In Jesus' Name, Amen.

A CLEAR COMMAND TO PRAY
Day 6 – Day 14

Seeing the people, He [Jesus] felt compassion for them,
because they were distressed and dispirited
like sheep without a shepherd.
Then He said to His disciples, "The harvest is plentiful
but the workers are few. Therefore beseech the Lord of the harvest
to send out workers into His harvest."
Matthew 9:36-38

Jesus told us to beseech the Lord of the harvest to send out workers.

What does it mean to *beseech*?
The word means to long for...to beg...to desire...to ask.
To pray.

How do we pray for this great need?
We don't have to figure it out for ourselves; the Word tells us plainly.
God commands us to pray, and He tells us how.

We just have to be willing to follow His instructions.

Day 6: Pray For Laborers

Take It In

Matthew 9:36-38 – *Seeing the people, He [Jesus] felt compassion for them, because they were distressed and dispirited like sheep without a shepherd. Then He said to His disciples, "The harvest is plentiful but the workers are few. Therefore beseech the Lord of the harvest to send out workers into His harvest."*

Think It Through

This is our Hebron. This is our kingdom work. Jesus challenges us to answer the call on our lives and obey His command. We've pulled up a chair to the King's table. We've entered the door of the sheepfold. The Shepherd has called our names and brought us into the pasture. Our future is set. Our hope is secure. Our identity is firmly grounded in Christ.

But what about the others? Do we have God's heart of compassion for those who haven't heard? Those who are distressed and dispirited? Look around you. You might be old. You might be weak and frail. You might have limitations. But this command is not dependent on your ability, but your availability. It's simply a matter of time and priority.

What does Jesus want us to do? *Ask His Father to send out workers into His harvest.* The harvest is a harvest of souls – people who will spend eternity separated from the God who loves them in a place of torment unless they come to Christ. It's your next-door neighbor. It's the cashier at Walmart. It's the guy who changes your oil. It's the person you'll never meet on the other side of the world. Jesus is telling us the field is huge and ready to be harvested, but there is a shortage of workers, and that's where you and I come in.

Are we to be workers in the harvest? Yes.
Are we to ask God to send others to the harvest? Yes.

In the very next chapter (Matthew 10), Jesus sends out His disciples to the surrounding villages and towns. They were responsible to go. But they were also responsible to ask God to send others, for the harvest is too great for a few. Do you see the beauty of God's eternal, enduring plan for an on-going harvest? We are always part of the harvest, but we are working in different places, at different times, and in different roles. At any point in time, some are laboring in the field, some are preparing for the field, and some are praying for others to be sent to the field.

Live It Out

Which person is more important – the person who gets on an airplane and lives in a foreign country, sharing the gospel with an unreached people group? Or the person giving generously to keep them on the field? Or is it the one who is laboring on their knees for God to strengthen and provide and empower, and asking for Him to send reinforcements?

The answer is that each one is indispensable, and God is not looking for comparison, but obedience.

What if no one went, but we all prayed?
What if no one gave, but we all went?
What if no one prayed, but we all gave?

God's economy of kingdom work is perfectly balanced and let's not forget – *He is the Lord of the harvest.* He determines when and where and how each of His children labor. As we obey and fulfill the role that He calls us to, the fields will be perfectly and fully harvested. After all, we know that it is His Spirit in us who is ultimately accomplishing the work. We are simply the vessels He uses.

If you've picked up this devotional, we believe it is because God is calling you to be part of a mighty army of prayer warriors. He is asking you to stop believing the lie that you are not valuable or useful anymore and start praying for laborers in the harvest. He is inviting you to labor for His kingdom and be a witness to the power of God for salvation for this generation. You may not be able to take a flight to a foreign country. You may not be able to prayer walk or attend a service or hand out tracts. You may rarely leave your home. But you can pray. You can pray for the power of God to move in His people and send out laborers for the harvest to come.

James 5:16b – *The effective prayer of a righteous man can accomplish much.*

Pray Today

Dear Father, You gave us a clear command to pray for laborers for the harvest. Some things in Your word are difficult to understand, but this is not one of them. Prayer is something that everyone of us can do, and you have uniquely positioned many of us in life so that prayer can become our passion. Help us to have compassionate hearts like Jesus and let that compassion and our desire to obey You become the catalyst for a mighty movement of prayer in our generation. In Jesus' Name, Amen.

Day 7: Pray God's Will

Take It In

1 John 5:14-15 – *This is the confidence which we have before Him, that, if we ask anything according to His will, He hears us. And if we know that He hears us in whatever we ask, we know that we have the requests which we have asked from Him.*

Think It Through

Have you ever prayed a prayer that God didn't seem to answer? Or that He answered, but not in the way you asked? If you've ever prayed at all, then most likely your answers are "yes!" Did this challenge your faith? Didn't Jesus tell us many times that whatever we ask in His name that God is sure to provide?

There are many reasons God chooses to answer our prayers in a way that we can't understand. He has all knowledge; He is sovereign; He desires the best for us; He has plans and purposes which we don't know yet. But in the scripture above, John tells us there is a way that our requests will always be heard by God, and that we can be assured of having what we ask for.

The secret is asking *according to His will.* The key, then, is to know His will, and this is something that even Jesus Himself had to leave in His Father's hands. In the Garden of Gethsemane, Jesus prayed for a different resolution to the problem of mankind's sinful state – any resolution except what He was facing on the cross. And as He poured out His heart to His Father, anxious and overwhelmed by what He knew was to come, He laid down His will and deferred to whatever His Father wanted. *Not My will, but Yours be done.* (Luke 22:42).

Jesus taught us by example that powerful, effective prayers are answered when we pray for God's will to be carried out. When we are assured of God's heart by His own words, then we can expect Him to answer our prayers.

Live It Out

In 1806, Samuel Mills, a Williams College student took God at His word and started what became known as the "Haystack Prayer Meeting." He and four other young men began praying that God would raise up men to take the gospel to the nations. At that time, American mission organizations were solely focused on domestic endeavors. This group of men were praying exactly what Jesus had asked: *for God to send laborers into the harvest.* History tells us that He answered those prayers exponentially beyond their imaginations, including the establishment of the American Board of Commissioners of Foreign Missions, the American Bible Society, and the United Foreign Missionary Society. Each of these organizations sent thousands to the field.

This gives us great assurance as we examine our call to pray for laborers for the harvest. Jesus Himself commanded us to pray this prayer. It is His will for God to move in believers' hearts and call them to go into the field and labor. We can pray passionately, confidently, and boldly, knowing that God is certain to not only hear our prayers, but to answer them in the affirmative!

Is this presuming on God?
Is this dictating our own will?

Not according to authority of scripture. Jesus has commanded us to pray for laborers. As we obey His command, we pray according to His will, and expect Him to answer.

Matthew 6:9-10 – *Pray, then, in this way: Our Father who is in heaven, hallowed be Your name. Your kingdom come, Your will be done, on earth as it is in heaven.*

Pray Today

Dear Father, We want to take You at Your word. We believe that You are Lord of the harvest, and that You are ready to call many laborers to the field. We ask You to send those laborers to our neighborhoods, our cities, our states, and our nation. We trust You to know when and where the laborers are needed, and for the harvest of lost souls that will be reaped. Because You have commanded us to ask for these laborers, we boldly pray in Jesus' name and believe You hear our prayers and will answer. In Jesus' Name, Amen.

DAY 8: PRAY PERSISTENTLY

Take It In

Luke 18:1-8 - *Now He was telling them a parable to show that at all times they ought to pray and not to lose heart, saying, "In a certain city there was a judge who did not fear God and did not respect man. There was a widow in that city, and she kept coming to him, saying, 'Give me legal protection from my opponent.' For a while he was unwilling; but afterward he said to himself, 'Even though I do not fear God nor respect man, yet because this widow bothers me, I will give her legal protection, otherwise by continually coming she will wear me out.'" And the Lord said, "Hear what the unrighteous judge said; now, will not God bring about justice for His elect who cry to Him day and night, and will He delay long over them? I tell you that He will bring about justice for them quickly. However, when the Son of Man comes, will He find faith on the earth?"*

1 Thessalonians 5:17 – *Pray without ceasing.*

Think It Through

This story makes me smile. Can't you see it? An arrogant judge with no respect for God or men is persistently pestered and continually badgered by a determined widow. She literally wore him down, not because of who she was, but because she persisted. She would not give up.

What gave her this confidence? First, she had a legal right to ask for the judge's help. Her request was according to the law, and the judge was obligated to respond. Second, she was not asking for special favors; she simply wanted justice. She wanted the outcome to be what the judge, as a representative of the law, should also want.

Why did Jesus tell this parable? He was revealing a secret of effective prayer: pray at all times, and don't lose heart.

To lose heart is to give up, faint, grow weary. It is to stop believing that our prayers make any difference. It is wanting to hold God accountable to our expectations and essentially declare, "Time's up! You didn't answer, so there's no use to keep praying!" Where's the faith in that approach?

Jesus is telling us that if an unrighteous human judge can be moved to do the right thing because of a persistent widow, how much more will His Father, the Righteous Judge, be moved by the persistent prayers of His elect! He is challenging us to know His Word and to pray persistently and continually if we want God to bring about justice.

Live It Out

At the end of the parable, Jesus asks a question. "When the Son of Man comes, will He find faith on the earth?" It takes great faith to pray persistently when we don't see God answering our prayers yet. The widow had great faith and persistence because she knew her own helplessness to solve the crisis. She could not protect herself legally. She was dependent on the judge to do the right thing on her behalf. Likewise, our faith grows as we recognize our dependence on God to accomplish the work. We are persistent because we are desperate. And we do not lose heart and give up because we trust the Righteous Judge to act.

We have confidence like the widow to pray continually and persistently because we are God's children. As we make it our passionate plea for the Lord of the Harvest to send out laborers for the gospel, we know we are asking for what is right and good, and what the Righteous Judge desires.

When it seems like God is not hearing you, don't lose heart. Jesus Himself said it: Keep on praying. Keep on asking. Pray persistently, and when He comes again, He will find you faithful.

Luke 11:5-9 - *Then He said to them, "Suppose one of you has a friend, and goes to him at midnight and says to him, 'Friend, lend me three loaves; for a friend of mine has come to me from a journey, and I have nothing to set before him'; and from inside he answers and says, 'Do not bother me; the door has already been shut and my children and I are in bed; I cannot get up and give you anything.' I tell you, even though he will not get up and give him anything because he is his friend, yet because of his persistence he will get up and give him as much as he needs. So I say to you, ask, and it will be given to you; seek, and you will find; knock, and it will be opened to you."*

Pray Today

Dear Father, We want to be like the persistent widow, and the persistent friend. We know You are a Righteous Judge, and You desire justice in the earth. Help us to pray persistently and not lose heart when it seems to us that You are not answering. Give us faith that pleases Jesus – faith that keeps on praying in the face of discouragement and doubt. And when You answer, let us be quick to praise You and share our stories to encourage others who may be disheartened. In Jesus' Name, Amen.

Day 9: Pray Boldly

Take It In

Ephesians 3:11-12 – *This was in accordance with the eternal purpose which He carried out in Christ Jesus our Lord, in whom we have boldness and confident access through faith in Him.*

Mark 11:22-24 – *And Jesus answered saying to them, "Have faith in God. Truly I say to you, whoever says to this mountain, 'Be taken up and cast into the sea,' and does not doubt in his heart, but believes that what he says is going to happen, it will be granted him. Therefore I say to you, all things for which you pray and ask, believe that you have received them, and they will be granted you.*

Think It Through

The passage in Mark is one that is often quoted but rarely believed. By that, I mean we encourage one another to pray bold prayers and believe God for the answer; but when it comes right down to it, we don't really believe we can have whatever we ask God for. How many times have we asked for Him to heal a loved one, and that loved one dies? How many times have we asked for Him to intervene, but circumstances don't change? How many times have we asked for a friend's salvation, but hearts remain hard and unyielding?

We talked about the guarantee for answered prayer a few days ago: *pray the will of God.* All of our prayers, all of our requests, and all of our pleas must have a conditional clause: if God wills, as God wills, and when God wills.

The principle that Jesus is teaching here is not that God will give us anything and everything we ask, but that we should pray bold prayers of faith, asking Him for the things *He* desires to do. You see, our boldness in prayer is directly related to our faith in the One to whom we pray. Paul says it in Ephesians: *we have boldness and confident access through faith in Him.*

Bold faith says, "Your will be done."
Bold faith says, "You will move the mountain according to Your plan."
Bold faith says, "I have all confidence in You, whatever You do."
Bold faith says, "I can approach God with any concern, and trust Him with the outcome."

Prayer that presumes on God to respond according to our expectation is not bold nor faith-filled because we are just asking for God to rubber stamp our own solution. We've already drawn our conclusions and come up with the answers. Instead, bold prayers bring the problem to God with open hands and hearts, and no expectations. It's saying to God, "Here's the mountain, and it needs to be moved, and I'm trusting You to move it in Your time and according to Your plan, because You see the whole picture."

Live It Out

What does the mountain represent? Is Jesus saying we can speak to a literal mountain and cast it into the sea? The word for mountain is *ores* and comes from a root word that means "to rise or rear." We use the phrase "move mountains" for anyone who accomplishes great or difficult things, despite obstacles which "rise up," impeding their progress. Jesus is telling us that nothing can prevent us from accomplishing the kingdom work that God has called us to do, and that all things can be overcome by faith in God. Before Jesus ever mentions moving the mountain, He tells us: *Have faith in God!*

What are we praying for? Is it for God's kingdom to come? For His will to be done? Then we can confidently believe that we have what we ask for. We can ask for it boldly, with our faith firmly centered on God, and wait expectantly for the mountain to move.

Mark 10:27 – *Looking at them, Jesus said, "With people it is impossible, but not with God; for all things are possible with God."*

Pray Today

Dear Father, You invite us to pray bold prayers. Not arrogant or brash demands for You to fulfill what we desire, but faith-filled, humble pleas for Your will to be done in our own lives, and in the lives of the people we love. Mountains will rise, and obstacles will come, but we can pray boldly for You to move those hindrances out of the way, so we can follow You more closely. Give us faith to pray bold prayers, but let our boldness be found in who You are, and not what You can do for us. In Jesus' Name, Amen.

DAY 10: PRAY SPECIFICALLY

Take It In

Colossians 4:2-4 – *Devote yourselves to prayer, keeping alert in it with an attitude of thanksgiving; praying at the same time for us as well, that God will open up to us a door for the word, so that we may speak forth the mystery of Christ, for which I have also been imprisoned; that I may make it clear in the way I ought to speak.*

Think It Through

If we want to know that God has answered our prayers, we must pray specifically. Paul is closing out his letter to the believers at the church in Colossae, and he asks them to pray for him. He makes a particular request; he wants more from them than just "God bless Paul." While God knows our hearts, and has already planned for our every need, there's something very precious and special about praying for one another in a specific, intimate way.

Paul's desire is for the gospel to be proclaimed, but he knows that unless God opens the door, all his preaching and teaching will be in vain. On one occasion, he desired to go to a place called Bithynia, but the Spirit of Jesus prevented him (Acts 16:7). He told the believers at Rome that he had often planned to visit them but had been prevented (Romans 1:13). He shares with the Corinthian church that he deliberately waited to visit, recognizing that their current spiritual condition would result in much sorrow, and perhaps a broken relationship. He waited, so that God would have time to prepare their hearts for the message of repentance He would bring (2 Corinthians 2:1-4).

Listen to how Paul describes the way God works in leading him to the places where the gospel would be received, even in the face of adversity:

Acts 14:27 – *They began to report all things that God had done with them and how He had opened a door of faith to the Gentiles.*

1 Corinthians 16:8-19 – *But I will remain in Ephesus until Pentecost; for a wide door for effective service has opened to me, and there are many adversaries.*

2 Corinthians 2:12-13 – *Now when I came to Troas for the gospel of Christ and when a door was opened for me in the Lord, I had no rest for my spirit, not finding Titus my brother; but taking my leave of them, I went on to Macedonia.*

You see, God knew every individual in each city and town where Paul was going. He was already at work in their hearts, preparing them to hear the gospel message that Paul would bring. By praying for open doors, and listening to God's Spirit to direct his steps, Paul maximized his ministry effectiveness. The gospel was shared at just the right time, in just the right place, and to just the right people.

Live It Out

Does God still do this today? What if we really believed that He has a sovereign plan for the gospel? What if we asked Him specifically to open the doors of our neighbors' homes so that the gospel could be shared? What if you prayed for my city, and I prayed for yours, much the same way that Paul asked the church at Colossae to pray for open doors all across Asia?

When we pray for open doors we are asking God to send laborers, messengers, and for His Spirit to do the work ahead of their arrival by opening hearts and spiritual eyes to receive the message. The wonderful thing about praying specifically for open doors is that we will know without a doubt God heard our prayers and answered them, as the gospel spreads!

Do you know of places in your city that need the gospel? Communities filled with people who speak another language, and worship other gods? Schools where teachers aren't allowed to share their faith? Parts of town you avoid because you know what happens there is dangerous or evil? Or maybe just down the street in your own neighborhood?

Pray for laborers to be sent. And pray specifically for open doors for the message of the gospel to be proclaimed and understood.

Ephesians 6:18-19 – *With all prayer and petition pray at all times in the Spirit, and with this in view, be on the alert with all perseverance and petition for all the saints, and pray on my behalf, that utterance may be given to me in the opening of my mouth, to make known with boldness the mystery of the gospel.*

Pray Today

Dear Father, What an honor we have to pray for open doors for the gospel, for in this way we are joining hands with You to accomplish what You desire the most – the redemption of Your people. Give us a passion to pray intentionally and specifically for the places around us. We ask for opportunities for Your laborers, and for open hearts and eyes to hear the good news about Jesus. In Jesus' Name, Amen.

DAY 11: PRAY SECRETLY

Take It In

Matthew 6:5-8 – *When you pray, you are not to be like the hypocrites; for they love to stand and pray in the synagogues and on the street corners so that they may be seen by men. Truly I say to you, they have their reward in full. But you, when you pray, go into your inner room, close your door and pray to your Father who is in secret, and your Father who sees what is done in secret will reward you. And when you are praying, do not use meaningless repetition as the Gentiles do, for they suppose that they will be heard for their many words. So do not be like them; for your Father knows what you need before you ask Him.*

Think It Through

With these simple instructions, Jesus dismantles everything about religion, and reminds us that His Father desires a relationship with us. He calls out the hypocrite who prays so that others will hear, and invites us to meet with God secretly, in our own private place, with no listening ears except for His.

What freedom! What intimacy! What assurance that God wants to hear from honest, open hearts. There is no need to worry about using the right words, or misquoting scripture, or praying something that sounds silly. There's no one to impress. The Father wants sincere conversation, not eloquent speeches.

What does praying in secret do for our prayer life?

It creates intimacy between us and God.

Jesus said our Father knows what we need before we ask Him; prayer is not about getting the right information to God, so He knows what decision to make. Prayer is the opportunity to express every feeling, every fear, every longing, every desire to the One who can help us. Have you ever had a burden that weighed you down until you simply had to talk to someone about it? We were made for community, and sharing our innermost thoughts is a relief. As we open ourselves up to God alone, His Spirit speaks to our spirit. He takes our burdens and concerns, our hopes, our fears upon Himself. We sense His love for us, and we can leave our cares with Him.

Casting all your anxiety on Him, because He cares for you. (1 Peter 5:7)

It grows our faith in God.

When we pray about something but tell no one else, and then see God answer that prayer in a specific, unmistakable way, our faith and confidence in Him grows in a manner that we can't experience any other way. Sometimes we pray with others, or in a worship service, lifting our needs to Him. And God answers, but there's always a human-thinking part of us that credits it to coincidence, or that someone just heard our prayers and acted on them. The reality is, God still answered it. But when we pray in secret and see God work, all doubts disappear, and we truly know He heard us!

In my trouble I cried to the Lord, and He answered me. (Psalm 120:1)

Live It Out

Is public prayer wrong? Is it offensive to God to write out a prayer and read it? Should we always pray alone? Jesus is not teaching against praying out loud or with others, for He often prayed so that others would hear. Praying with other Christ-followers encourages and comforts us. Mature saints have a lifetime of experience and familiarity with the Father and listening to an older believer pray can bless and teach a younger believer as they learn.

Jesus is offering us the opportunity to experience prayer for what it truly is: an intimate time of sharing our hearts with the One who knows us best. No need to worry if we're saying the wrong thing, or if anyone else will think we are weak or foolish. No one to be offended by our prayers for their salvation. No ears to hear our concerns for their spiritual condition. Just you and the Father, in tune with each other's heart, His Spirit guiding your thoughts and your spirit responding in prayer.

Matthew 14:23 - *After [Jesus] had sent the crowds away, He went up on the mountain by Himself to pray; and when it was evening, He was there alone.*

Pray Today

Dear Father, Thank You for inviting us to pray in secret. You strip away all the things that don't matter when it's just the two of us. You don't need fancy words, and it doesn't matter what anyone else thinks. You only want us to be sincere and honest, sharing the deepest thoughts in our hearts which You already know anyway. Teach us to trust You with our hearts and let us enjoy the reward of intimacy with You as we learn to pray in secret. In Jesus' Name, Amen.

DAY 12: PRAY GRATEFULLY

Take It In

1 Thessalonians 5:16-18 – *Rejoice always; pray without ceasing; in everything give thanks; for this is God's will for you in Christ Jesus.*

Think It Through

We often read Paul's instructions in 1 Thessalonians as separate statements:

Rejoice always.
Pray without ceasing.
In everything give thanks.

But look again – it is one sentence, one command which describes God's will for us in Christ Jesus. The joy of knowing Christ results in unceasing prayer, which overflows in thanksgiving. These are not tasks to accomplish. These are the attitudes of our hearts (joy and gratitude) that can't be contained and find their source in abiding in Christ. How else could we "pray without ceasing?"

There is a joy in praying to our Heavenly Father knowing that whatever the answer is, it will be good. James reminds us that *every good thing given and every perfect gift is from above, coming down from the Father of lights, with whom there is no variation or shifting shadow* (James 1:17). God is not playing tricks on us; **everything** He gives is good.

When we pray from a heart of gratitude, we are letting our Father know that we trust Him to answer for our good. An ungrateful heart says, "I must have this to be happy." A true heart of thankfulness recognizes the hand of the Giver, and surrenders to His will, no matter how difficult or painful the answer may be. We trust His all-knowing heart of love, and thank Him for it, no matter what "it" may be.

Live It Out

How does a heart of gratitude change our prayers for the spread of the gospel? We are thankful for that cranky neighbor who irritates us, because their presence in our lives causes us to run to the Father and ask for His grace and love to share. *Oh, now we see!* He fills our hearts with His love and grace, and the cranky neighbor becomes the conduit through which we experience the presence of God in our own lives.

We are thankful for the awkwardness when we struggle to speak the words of the gospel to the person God puts in front of us, because it causes us to depend on the Spirit to empower our weak words and bring thoughts to our minds. *Oh, now we see!* He uses us as His messenger despite our awkwardness and we delight in realizing He has spoken through us!

We are thankful when we are overwhelmed by the sheer numbers of people who are lost and separated without God because it drives us to our knees to ask the Father of the harvest to send out laborers. *Oh, now we see!* We are filled with joy to read the stories of those who have been sent, knowing that we have been part of their effectiveness on the field through our prayers!

We are thankful when our hearts are broken for family members who continue to reject the truth and are bound by chains of destruction because we recognize how dependent we are on the power of God to change us. *Oh, now we see!* We are filled with humility and overwhelmed by the grace of God that He saw fit to open our eyes, and we pray unceasingly for those who cannot see.

What are you grateful for today? How will it change your prayers?

Philippians 4:6 – *Be anxious for nothing, but in everything by prayer and supplication with thanksgiving let your requests be made known to God.*

Pray Today

Dear Father, How much we have to be grateful for! If only we will stop and think about it. You are a God who hears our prayers and promises only good. Teach us to trust Your heart, even when we cannot understand the work that You are doing. Open our eyes to the spiritual, so that we can live gratefully, pray gratefully, and gratefully share the truth about You with a world that is living in spiritual darkness. Let our prayers always begin with "thank You" before we ever ask You for anything else. In Jesus' Name, Amen.

Day 13: Pray In The Spirit

Take It In

Ephesians 6:18 – *With all prayer and petition pray at all times in the Spirit, and with this in view, be on the alert with all perseverance and petition for all the saints.*

Romans 8:26-27 – *In the same way the Spirit also helps our weakness; for we do not know how to pray as we should, but the Spirit Himself intercedes for us with groanings too deep for words; and He who searches the hearts knows what the mind of the Spirit is, because He intercedes for the saints according to the will of God.*

Think It Through

What does it mean to "pray in the Spirit?" Is it an experience to be sought after, a mystical trance, or an out-of-body encounter? Is it just for a few, select believers who can achieve a special status? No, Paul is speaking to every believer who possesses the indwelling Spirit of God. Earlier in Romans 8, he reminds us that if the Spirit does not dwell in us, we do not belong to God. If you belong to Christ, then you are to pray in the Spirit.

Paul uses this phrase two times in the New Testament. In Ephesians 6, the context is spiritual warfare. He has given us our spiritual clothing and our weapons: the full armor of God. We stand firm, clothed in truth, righteousness, and the gospel. We take up our shield of faith and put on the helmet of salvation. Then he gives us the key to praying in the Spirit: the sword of the Spirit, which is the **word of God.**

We pray in the Spirit when we pray according to the word of God, and most powerfully when we pray God's word back to Him. We speak truth, claiming the promises of God. We remind Him of His covenant with us and ask Him to fulfill His sovereign purposes in whatever situation we face. We pray for one another, speaking His word over each other, whether it is encouragement, comfort, or truth told in love. We agree with God by verbalizing what He has already said. When we pray according to the word, we are praying for God's will to be done; this gives us confidence that He hears our prayers.

Paul commands us to intercede for one another. The Spirit is the One who does this, as we see in Romans 8. When we don't know how to pray or what to pray, the Spirit of God is already interceding on our behalf. He searches our hearts, brings scripture to our minds and reminds us of what God has said (John 14:26). The Holy Spirit knows the will of God and the mind of God, and He speaks into our heart so that we will *pray in the Spirit.*

Live It Out

How can we grow in our practice of "praying in the Spirit?" We do not have the power to make the Spirit speak to us, but we do have the choice to give Him the opportunity. The first requirement is time. God speaks on His timetable, not ours. Secondly, we must listen, and this means we must be quiet. A quiet place. A quiet mind. We must silence our voices so that we can hear His. And we must pray with our Bibles open, reading His word so that He can speak through it.

My husband tells the story of being alone one day while reading and studying the Bible. He began praying for our neighbors, and while he was praying, the Spirit of God impressed upon his heart that his prayers were too limited. We were developing a ministry which has a vision is to "take the gospel to every neighborhood in America," yet we were only praying for those right around us. He began to pray for the believers he knew in other cities and states, asking God to stir their hearts for the gospel. Before he knew it, an hour had passed, and he had traveled all across the country in his prayers. It was a divine, Spirit-led, time of praying in the Spirit, and it refreshed his soul and renewed him.

Times like my husband experienced do not have to be few and far between, but I fear they are because we are simply too noisy and too busy to experience them. May all of us learn what it means to pray in the Spirit and be willing to sacrifice what is necessary to experience Him.

Jude 1:20-21 – *But you, beloved, building yourselves up on your most holy faith, praying in the Holy Spirit, keep yourselves in the love of God, waiting anxiously for the mercy of our Lord Jesus Christ to eternal life.*

Pray Today

Dear Father, Oh how we long to experience You in our times of prayer! Simply praying in our own strength and knowledge is not enough. We want Spirit-empowered prayer that moves mountains and defeats our enemy. Teach us to be quiet. Teach us to listen, and to hear You speak through Your word. Show us what it means to pray Your word over one another and let us experience the refreshing of our souls which only comes from being in Your presence. In Jesus' Name, Amen.

DAY 14: PRAY WITH A PURE HEART

Take It In

2 Chronicles 7:14 – *And My people who are called by My name humble themselves and pray and seek My face and turn from their wicked ways, then I will hear from heaven, will forgive their sin and will heal their land.*

Psalm 66:18 – *If I regard wickedness in my heart, the Lord will not hear.*

Think It Through

Are there times when you feel as though your prayers are bouncing off the ceiling? Have you started to believe that God isn't listening at all, and that praying is a futile effort? When this happens, we usually blame God, that He doesn't care anymore. But Solomon's experience reveals that we need to examine ourselves.

When God made the promise in 2 Chronicles 7:14, He was responding to Solomon's prayer of dedication for the temple. Solomon asked for God's presence in the midst of the people, for the temple to be a place where God's Shekinah glory would rest, and that His eyes and ears would always be open to the people's prayers. This is a beautiful and expressive prayer of humility, and in it, Solomon mentions all the ways and reasons the Jewish people might fail God. Eight times he pleads that God would still **hear from heaven** and **forgive** and **act** in His righteousness, mercy and justice on behalf of the people (2 Chronicles 6:12-42).

God's response shows us that the state of our hearts has an impact on whether He will hear us. He promises to listen to the prayers of a pure heart.

How do we know if our heart is pure? As a New Testament believer, our sins have been forgiven, including past, present and future sins. In Christ, our spirits are already pure and holy, destined for eternal life.

Our physical bodies, however, are still unredeemed. Our fleshly desires and human thinking can lead us astray. Our hearts can deceive us, and as Solomon reminded us in his prayer, *when they sin against You (for there is no man who does not sin)*, we all sin even as born-again believers (2 Chronicles 6:36). God knows this and gives us three words that define the heart that pleases Him, and whose prayers He hears:

A pure heart is **humble**.
A pure heart is **persistent**.
A pure heart is **repentant**.

Live It Out

Notice that God did not say He hears the prayers of the perfect heart. If that were true, we all should give up praying. God is not looking for perfection, but for purity. A man with a pure heart humbles himself, recognizing and acknowledging his own sinful choices. He does not ask for forgiveness in a flippant or meaningless way, but seeks God's face, desperate for the Father's grace and mercy. He understands his sin grieves God's heart. He turns away from any known sin, whether it is an outward act of disobedience, an ungrateful thought, or a complaining heart that is chafing against the trials and tribulations of life.

A pure heart exposes its own need of God, and prays the prayer that God hears and forgives. It is a prayer that moves God to act in mercy, grace, righteousness and justice.

As we pray for the gospel to spread from neighborhoods to nations, we must examine our own hearts first. Let us be people who are humble. Let us be persistent in seeking God's face. And let us repent when He convicts us so that we can pray with confidence and power, knowing that He will hear. After all, the lost world is desperate for God to answer.

1 Peter 3:12 – *For the eyes of the Lord are toward the righteous, and His ears attend to their prayer, but the face of the Lord is against those who do evil.*

Pray Today

Dear Father, How many times do we allow the trivial and petty things of life to harden our hearts, and miss the bounty and beauty of answered prayer? How many times do we come into Your throne room trailing the dirt of our disobedience and wearing the stains of the world, too self-absorbed to recognize that our sins offend and grieve You? Forgive us for our proud hearts and unrepentant thoughts. We ask for Your Spirit to convict us so that we can come to You with pure hearts, for the needs of our world are great, and you have called us to intercede for a lost world. Let us never forget what is at stake. In Jesus' Name, Amen.

A Proven Pattern Of Prayer
Day 15 – Day 20

Now these things happened to them as an example,
and they were written for our instruction,
upon whom the ends of the ages have come.
1 Corinthians 10:11

God gives us a pattern for prayer in the words of His faithful
servants which are preserved in scripture for our benefit.

Pray honestly and humbly, like Job.
Pray boldly, like Paul.
Pray from a heart of worship, like Anna.
Pray in dependence and desperation, like Moses.

And for a simple pattern of prayer that touches the Father's heart,
learn to pray like Jesus.

What pattern of prayer will you leave those who come behind you?

DAY 15: PRAY LIKE ANNA

Take It In

Luke 2:36-38 – *And there was a prophetess, Anna the daughter of Phanuel, of the tribe of Asher. She was advanced in years and had lived with her husband seven years after her marriage, and then as a widow to the age of eighty-four. She never left the temple, serving night and day with fastings and prayers. At that very moment she came up and began giving thanks to God, and continued to speak of Him to all those who were looking for the redemption of Jerusalem.*

Think It Through

Anna is a great example to all of us, no matter what age we are. After all, she'd made it a lifetime habit to be in a spirit of worship. *She never left the temple.*

That sounds strange to us, doesn't it? We struggle to get to church once a week, let alone for Wednesday prayer meeting, or any other special events! I don't believe this means she actually lived at the temple but indicates she made serving and worshipping God the total focus of her life as a widow. Surely this was not the life she anticipated as a new bride. She had expected to live out her days loving her husband, as any young Jewish girl in those days would envision. But God had a different plan for her life. He called her as a prophetess and settled her in a place of service that was close to His heart – that of prayer and fasting. What can we learn from Anna?

She was faithful to her calling.

As a prophetess, Anna would have been speaking about the coming Messiah, for that was the very heart of all the prophecies. If she had married as a young girl, perhaps sixteen, and lived with her husband seven years, she had served as a prophetess for at least sixty years! She never stopped looking for the promised Messiah!

How many of us would have lost faith?
How many of us would have turned away?

She was persistent in her prayers.

Night and day. Every day. She believed the Messiah would come, and she prayed for God to send Him. She had hope and confidence in the promises of God.

How many of us would have given up?
How many of us would have felt God had misled us?

She was sacrificial in her worship.

Not only was Anna faithful to her calling as a prophetess, and persistent in her prayers, she was willing to sacrifice as an act of worship. She fasted regularly and often, and her fasts were simply an overflow of the sacrifice of her life given to serve God in His temple.

How many of us would sacrifice our lives?
How many of us would sacrifice a meal?

Live It Out

Anna's faithfulness was rewarded. By her obedience and commitment, God sovereignly allowed her to be in just the right place at just the right time. She was present when Mary and Joseph brought the infant Jesus into the temple to be presented to God, according to their Jewish customs. I believe she overheard Simeon's blessing, and at that moment realized that all her prayers, all her fasting, all her prophecies, and indeed, the very sacrifice of her life came to its glorious fulfillment. She gazed on the Messiah, the Son of God, and gave thanks.

What is it that God has called you to do? Is He stirring up your heart to be part of a great army of prayer warriors, to fast and pray and sacrifice your time and energy for a holy service? Will you be like Anna, and pray persistently and faithfully, with a heart of sacrificial worship?

1 Timothy 2:8, 5:5 – *Therefore I want the men in every place to pray, lifting up holy hands, without wrath and dissension. ... Now she who is a widow indeed and who has been left alone, has fixed her hope on God and continues in entreaties and prayers night and day.*

Pray Today

Dear Father, We ask You to make us faithful prayer warriors like Anna. Let us never give up and never lose heart, and may we be willing to spend our very lives in worship and anticipation of seeing Jesus, with a hunger for You above all else. In Jesus' Name, Amen.

Day 16: Pray Like Job

Take It In

Job 42:1-6 – *Then Job answered the Lord and said, "I know that You can do all things, and that no purpose of Yours can be thwarted. Who is this that hides counsel without knowledge? Therefore I have declared that which I did not understand, things too wonderful for me, which I did not know. Hear, now, and I will speak; I will ask You, and You instruct me. I have heard of You by the hearing of the ear; but now my eye sees You; therefore I retract, and I repent in dust and ashes."*

Think It Through

I read a book a few years ago that was composed entirely of letters. The story unfolded through short notes and lengthy discourses from each character. Through the letters, I was able to follow the story of their lives. Each person's correspondence revealed both the actual events as well as their inner thoughts and feelings about each other and what was happening to them. It's an interesting way to enjoy a story.

The book of Job is similar. We are given a peek into conversations between God and Satan, God and Job, and Job and his four friends. Job's trials begin when Satan confronts God, accusing Job of being faithful only because he is blessed and protected. God allows Satan to attack Job's possessions, his family, and his health. We have the insight of the "prequel" to Job's suffering, and we know why it happened; the author of the book had Spirit-revealed knowledge. But Job suffered in the dark, not understanding why God had apparently turned against him, tearing away the very fabric of his life.

If you want the whole picture, you must read the whole story, and even then, it is difficult to decide whose explanations for this turn of events in Job's life are to be believed. His four friends, Eliphaz, Bildad, Zophar and Elihu all assume that there must be sin in Job's life. Defending himself, Job continues to declare his integrity and innocence. In the end, God reveals that Job's friends got it wrong, but that Job had some things to learn as well.

Live It Out

Like Job, we may face trials and suffering that we simply do not understand. We spend our lives living as faithfully as we possibly can. We give to the poor. We defend the weak and afflicted. We speak truth and wisdom. We keep our hearts pure and live with integrity. Then suddenly, out of nowhere, we face indescribable, distressing and heartbreaking events. We lose our health. We lose our loved ones. We lose our reputation. And when we cry out like Job, asking God to give a reason for our pain, we find Him silent, and are left with the platitudes and assumptions of well-meaning friends.

In those times, we can pray like Job. He demonstrates an intimacy and connection with God that allowed him to be open, vulnerable and truthful with his Father. He held nothing back. He expressed his pain and his confusion, trusting that God was able to handle it. But there was a maturity and wisdom in his prayers throughout the book, seen in three truths that help us keep a proper perspective in our prayers while suffering.

Job had an enduring faith in the midst of his questioning.
Though He slay me, I will hope in Him. Nevertheless I will argue my ways before Him. (13:15)

Job had an eternal perspective as he faced his own mortality.
As for me, I know that my Redeemer lives, and at the last He will take His stand on the earth. Even after my skin is destroyed, yet from my flesh I shall see God; whom I myself shall behold, and whom my eyes will see and not another. My heart faints within me! (19:25-27)

Job had an expectant humility as he waited for God to act.
Then Job answered the Lord and said, "Behold, I am insignificant; what can I reply to You? I lay my hand on my mouth. Once I have spoken, and I will not answer; even twice, and I will add nothing more." (40:3-5)

Job teaches us that it is not wrong to wrestle with God in prayer. It is in the wrestling we may truly come to see Him as sovereign and wise. We then realize that though we may be faithful followers, God has more to do in our hearts and lives. Let us not be afraid to be honest with God, but in our honesty, we must remember that He is our Creator and our Lord. He has all authority and right to do with us as He desires, and in the end, we will see His glory.

Pray Today

Dear Father, The most painful part of Job's story is that he didn't know why. But when we don't know the "why" of our troubles we can still have confidence in the "Who" – You! Like Job, we recognize that we have limited knowledge. Your thoughts are higher, and Your plans are greater, and we can trust You with today just as we trust You with our eternity. Teach us to pray honestly and intimately, and then leave the results to You. In Jesus' Name, Amen.

Day 17: Pray Like Paul

Take It In

Ephesians 3:14-21 – *For this reason I bow my knees before the Father, from whom every family in heaven and on earth derives its name, that He would grant you, according to the riches of His glory, to be strengthened with power through His Spirit in the inner man, so that Christ may dwell in your hearts through faith; and that you, being rooted and grounded in love, may be able to comprehend with all the saints what is the breadth and length and height and depth, and to know the love of Christ which surpasses knowledge, that you may be filled up to all the fullness of God. Now to Him who is able to do far more abundantly beyond all that we ask or think, according to the power that works within us, to Him be the glory in the church and in Christ Jesus to all generations forever and ever. In Jesus' Name, Amen.*

Think It Through

Paul's prayer for the Ephesian believers comes just after his explanation of the miraculous things God has done for us in salvation. He has reminded us of the great divide between men and God that has been crossed – something only God could do. He has given us tangible examples to explain the unique relationship we now have with God, and with each other. His description of our "before" (dead, wrath, separate, far off, no hope, enmity, strangers, aliens) contrasts sharply with our "after" (blessed, chosen, lavished with grace, sealed, God's own possession, a body, alive, raised up, brought near, reconciled, fellow citizens, saints, a holy temple).

As he starts to pray at the beginning of the third chapter in his letter, *For this reason,* he seems to interrupt himself and go off on another subject (3:1,14). But I believe he realized he needed to give a framework to the prayer that was stirring in his heart. He shares the mission and ministry that God has given to him personally: to proclaim the mystery of the gospel to the Gentiles. It is this mission that fuels the powerful words he prays over his fellow believers.

Paul's passion for the gospel causes him to pray four specific things for those who share his faith, and his obedience to Jesus' command to go and make disciples.

He prays for believers to be strengthened by the power of the Holy Spirit.

The spread of the gospel is a work of the Spirit. Our words must be empowered by Him, and our actions must be prompted by Him.

He prays for believers to be assured of their own salvation.
Until we are confident and grounded in our own conversion to Christ, we will never be bold witnesses. We cannot preach what we do not believe.

He prays for believers to be saturated with God's love.
Paul knows by personal experience that talking about Jesus in a hostile, ungodly world is to guarantee rejection, even the risking of our lives. Unless we are rooted in God's love, and know personally how wide, how high, how long and how deep that love is not only for us, but for the world, we will give up. Our fleshly strength and good deeds will not last; we must be fueled by the very love of God.

He prays for believers to expect supernatural results.
Paul encourages us to believe God for things we can't even imagine; things like the salvation of the person we believed could never change. The hardest heart is not beyond the "power that works within us" because that power is the Spirit of the God who created the world and set it in motion. It accomplishes the impossible.

Live It Out

To pray like Paul is to pray for others to experience the same amazing grace and salvation that we ourselves have experienced. It is to pray that our neighbors, our co-workers, our friends and our families will be touched by the power of God, as God uses us to share the good news about Jesus. And the result? Well, Paul says it this way: *Glory in the church and in Christ Jesus to all generations.* Our prayers can influence others, not just in our lifetime, but they can have an impact for God's glory for generations after us! Let's pray like Paul, expecting God to do great things to change our world for His glory.

2 Corinthians 8:23 - *As for Titus, he is my partner and fellow worker among you; as for our brethren, they are messengers of the churches, a glory to Christ.*

Pray Today

Dear Father, Teach us to pray powerful prayers like Paul. We want to influence our world with Your gospel, and see that influence carry on through many generations. We believe You can do things beyond our expectations and ask You to use our prayers for Your glory. In Jesus' Name, Amen.

DAY 18: PRAY LIKE ELIJAH

Take It In

James 5:16b-18 – *The effective prayer of a righteous man can accomplish much. Elijah was a man with a nature like ours, and he prayed earnestly that it would not rain, and it did not rain on the earth for three years and six months. Then he prayed again, and the sky poured rain and the earth produced its fruit.*

Think It Through

At first read, you might think this verse indicates that we must discover the "right" way to pray to be effective; that a prayer that is effective has something to do with us and how we pray. It's actually the other way around. Prayer has an effect on the righteous man.

The Greek word for effective is *energeō*, from which we get our word "energy." It means to be at work in or put forth power. The same word is used in Philippians 2:13, where Paul tells us *it is God who is at **work** in you, both to will and to **work** for His good pleasure.* The root of this word, *energēs*, appears in Hebrews 4:12, where we learn that *the word of God is living and **active [powerful]** and sharper than any two-edged sword.*

Prayer works in us. It produces an effect in the righteous, praying man, to bring him into line with the will of God. We see this in Elijah's life. It was God's will to withhold rain from the land of Israel in punishment for their idol worship under Ahab and Jezebel. Elijah had no power to keep back the rain, but as he prayed earnestly, his thoughts were brought in line with God's plan. The result was that Elijah could boldly say to Ahab, "It's not going to rain until I say so!" (1 Kings 17:1)

Three and a half years later, we see Elijah still praying according to God's will in his public battle with Baal on Mount Carmel. After the prophets of Baal had cried out all day with no answer, Elijah commands the Lord's sacrifice to be soaked with water three times, and then prays boldly, publicly:

O Lord, the God of Abraham, Isaac and Israel, today let it be known that You are God in Israel and that I am Your servant and I have done all these things at Your word. Answer me, O Lord, answer me, that this people may know that You, O Lord, are God, and that You have turned their heart back again. (1 Kings 18:36b-37)

Live It Out

Elijah's prayer on Mount Carmel reveals the work of God in his heart.

He magnified God as the one true God of Israel.
He acknowledged himself as the servant of God, bowing to His will.
He declared his obedience to God's commands.
He revealed his true motives: for the people to recognize God, repent, and turn back to Him.

Our prayers are effective when they cause us to see who God is and create in our hearts a fervent desire to obey Him and surrender to His will. This is the "much" that is accomplished, according to James. God doesn't need our prayers to advance His will. He is sovereign Lord over all. No purpose of His can be thwarted (Job 42:2); no one can ward off His hand, but He does as He wills (Daniel 4:35). It has far less to do with the actual outcome or answer that we seek, and much more to do with the work that He is doing inside of us.

To pray like Elijah is to seek after God Himself in total dependence, recognizing that we have no power in our prayers no matter how fervently we pray. The power is in the surrender of our will to the work of God in us, and as we spend time with Him, we will hear His heart and our prayers will be effective.

Ephesians 3:20 – *Now to Him who is able to do far more abundantly beyond all that we ask or think, according to the power that works within us.*

Pray Today

Dear Father, How easy it is for us think that prayer is about accomplishing something, or getting something, or changing something we do not like in our lives. The truth is, prayer is about You. It's about surrendering ourselves, not asserting our wills. Help us to be like Elijah and keep our lives free from sin so that we can pray fervently as righteous people. May the fervor of our prayers create willing hearts and minds that are fully given to obeying You, desiring only Your will to be accomplished. In Jesus' Name, Amen.

DAY 19: PRAY LIKE MOSES

Take It In

Exodus 33:12-15 – *Then Moses said to the Lord, "See, You say to me, 'Bring up this people!' But You Yourself have not let me know whom You will send with me. Moreover, You have said, 'I have known you by name, and you have also found favor in My sight.' Now therefore, I pray You, if I have found favor in Your sight, let me know Your ways that I may know You, so that I may find favor in Your sight. Consider too, that this nation is Your people." And He said, "My presence shall go with you, and I will give you rest." Then he said to Him, "If Your presence does not go with us, do not lead us up from here."*

Think It Through

Moses had a tough job to do! Even though he had been raised as an Egyptian prince, full of confidence and authority, his "training time" as a shepherd on the back side of the desert had humbled him. He was no longer confident in his own abilities, and when God called him to confront Pharaoh and lead the children of Israel out of slavery, he was so nervous he begged God to send someone along with him to speak (Exodus 3-4). It was not a stellar beginning for a hero of the faith. But something changed in Moses as he surrendered his will and obeyed God. He had the incredible privilege of seeing miracle after miracle happen, even using his own hands and words to showcase the amazing, supernatural power of God. Moses learned firsthand that it didn't matter how weak or incapable or nervous he was; if he simply surrendered and obeyed, God would be glorified.

The prayer of Moses in Exodus 33 comes on the heels of a great time of shame for the people of Israel. Moses had been with God for forty days. The people watched him walk up the trail into what looked like a terrible thunderstorm on the top of the mountain. They were full of fear before he left, and with no sign of his return, they went to Aaron and asked him to make them a god. After all, no one knew what had happened to Moses, and if they were going to survive they needed supernatural help. Aaron, bless his heart, showed little spiritual leadership. He asked the people to give him all their gold jewelry, and he fashioned a golden calf out of the melted materials. He set it before them and the people proclaimed it to be their god. Aaron built an altar, and they made burnt offerings to the calf, and spent the day eating, drinking, and mocking God. This is the scene Moses walked into as he descended from the mountain. Before he ever reached the bottom, God, knowing what was happening, told him that He was so angry He was ready to destroy the entire nation and start over with Moses! Moses interceded, reminding God that if He destroys Israel, it is His name that will be mocked by the Egyptians, claiming that God brought them out to kill them. He reminded God of His covenant promises to Abraham, Isaac and Jacob, and asked for mercy. God relented, and the people were not destroyed, although 3,000 of the Israelites died in punishment for their sin of idol worship.

God tells Moses to go up to the promised land but says He will not be going with them. He offers to send an angel before them, to help drive out their enemies, but because of the people's obstinate disobedience, He will let them go without Him, so that He will not destroy them on the way. Can you see how passionate God is? He loves this people, but their sin offends Him so deeply, He doesn't want to be with them.

Live It Out

Moses is devastated to think that God will not join them on the journey, for he knows that without God, they are lost. His prayer is a plea for God's presence. He knows the Lord so intimately that he would rather walk in fear of God's righteous anger than to go it alone. He trusts God's heart more than he trusts in himself, and he recognizes that they need God's presence if they want to become the people of God.

How often do we accept a task that God has given us but forget that we need His presence with us to accomplish it? When God allows us to experience a time of waiting, do we rush to fill His place with other things, other plans, other gods? Or do we realize that without His presence and leading, all our efforts are in vain?

As we learn to pray for the gospel to be proclaimed, let's pray like Moses. When God disciplines us for our own good, let us lean into the assurance of our covenant salvation and trust His heart. Let us realize that unless He goes with us, we will not succeed, and pray diligently for His favor and presence.

Psalm 33:18 – *Behold, the eye of the Lord is on those who fear Him, on those who hope for His lovingkindness.*

Pray Today

Dear Father, As we learn to trust Your heart, we long for Your presence. No matter how hard the task is, or how many times we fail, we would rather have You on our side than try to live on our own. Moses taught us that we can trust You even when You discipline us, and that Your heart is for Your covenant people. May we always be desperately dependent on You. In Jesus' Name, Amen.

Day 20: Pray Like Jesus

Take It In

Matthew 6:7-13 – *And when you are praying, do not use meaningless repetition as the Gentiles do, for they suppose that they will be heard for their many words. So do not be like them; for your Father knows what you need before you ask Him. Pray then, in this way: "Our Father who is in heaven, hallowed be Your name. Your kingdom come. Your will be done, on earth as it is in heaven. Give us this day our daily bread. And forgive us our debts, as we also have forgiven our debtors. And do not lead us into temptation, but deliver us from evil. For Yours is the kingdom and the power and the glory forever. Amen."*

Think It Through

These verses in Matthew are commonly known as "The Lord's Prayer" and have been repeated by believers and unbelievers alike ever since they were written down by Matthew. Jesus must have known the impact these words would have, so He forewarned us not to let them become a *meaningless repetition*. Whenever we pray, our hearts and minds must be fully engaged on the meaning of what we are saying. Jesus gave us not only a prayer to repeat, but a pattern to follow in all our prayers.

Here are six things Jesus teaches us about prayer.

We enter God's presence as family.
Jesus tells us to approach God as our Father. This immediately brings us into a sense of intimacy, care, provision, and security – all the things that a perfect Father would provide. In Christ, we are loved and welcomed as family.

We approach God in awe of Who He is.
God is our Father, but He also is the Creator and Sustainer of everything. Yes, we are family, but we recognize that He is "hallowed" (set apart, holy). Not only is He Himself holy, His very name is holy, and we speak to Him in humility, wonder, respect, and awe.

We submit to His will and seek His desires.
Whatever it is that we are asking God for must be surrendered to His will and for His kingdom purposes. In other words, we can ask Him for many things, but with the stipulation that we want it only as it brings honor, attention, and glory to Him, and accomplishes His perfect and sovereign will.

We express complete and constant dependence on Him.
Daily bread means that we only ask God for what we need today and trust Him for tomorrow's need. It also means that we come daily, showing a dependence not only on His provision, but His presence. Prayer is simply spending time in His presence, and a daily dependence delights His heart and teaches us to trust.

We experience forgiveness because we repent.
Jesus warns that if we fail to forgive others, God will not forgive us (Matthew 6:14-15). We know that we are fully forgiven at salvation but living with a forgiving spirit towards others makes us aware of our own sin and need for God's patience and tolerance when we fail. Harboring a grudge is a sin, and sin breaks our fellowship with God. As we repent and confess our sins, we are filled with the desire to restore our relationships with others.

We appeal for His sovereign direction and protection.
James 1 assures us that God does not tempt anyone to sin, but that He will allow trials to test and prove our faith. Jesus teaches us to ask God to protect us in those trials, that we do not fall into sin and be drawn away from Him. We trust God to know the future, and we pray for Him to guide our steps toward holiness, not failure.

Live It Out

A prayer life that includes these six elements results in a proper perspective of God. Our prayers will end in heart-felt **praise**, as seen in Jesus' closing words. We realize *the kingdom belongs to God forever, the power belongs to God forever, and the glory belongs to God forever!*

Jesus gave us a pattern that leads our hearts to recognize how holy the Father is, how able He is to meet our needs and direct our steps, how intimately He delights in us, and how powerfully He acts for our good and His glory. In every element, the focus is adjusting our thoughts to His, and expressing complete dependence on Him.

How will you pray like Jesus today?

Pray Today

Dear Father, How awesome and holy You are! We recognize our dependence on You and ask for Your guidance and protection as we seek to live our lives to reflect Your glory. We trust You. In Jesus' Name, Amen!

THE POWER OF PRAYER
Day 21 – Day 25

I pray that the eyes of your heart may be enlightened,
so that you will know what is the hope of His calling,
what are the riches of the glory of His inheritance in the saints,
and what is the surpassing greatness of His power toward us who believe.
Ephesians 1:18-19a

There is power in prayer, but the source of this power is not in our words,
or in our ability to be eloquent. The power is in the One to whom we pray.

It is a power with surpassing greatness.
It is a power that moves on our behalf, toward those who believe.
It is the same power that raised Christ from the dead.

What challenge do you face that is greater than death?
What could possibly limit you more than death?

Prayer that finds its hope in a powerful God can
defeat every enemy,
free every captive,
overcome every temptation,
fill us with joy,
and carry on the work that Jesus came to do.

DAY 21: PRAYER CONTINUES JESUS' WORK

Take It In

John 14:12-14 – *Truly, truly, I say to you, he who believes in Me, the works that I do, he will do also; and greater works than these he will do; because I go to the Father. Whatever you ask in My name, that will I do, so that the Father may glorified in the Son. If you ask Me anything in My name, I will do it.*

Think It Through

John 14-17 contain Jesus' last words to His disciples before He went to the cross. He sat with them at the Passover table and revealed important truths that would sustain them through His crucifixion, burial, resurrection, and return to His Father. Literally, they were His dying words, as if on this last special night together, when He knew that nothing would ever be the same, He poured out the secrets of kingdom life and described the joyful relationship that would be theirs when the Spirit came to indwell.

The disciples had experienced a relationship with Jesus unlike any other. They had talked face to face with the Son of God, trailed along as He performed miracles, and been questioned and ostracized for associating with Him. They had received "insider information" as He spoke in parables to the people but shared the heavenly meanings to them in private. Now He was passing His mission to them. He would no longer walk the earth, teaching, preaching and healing, but they would go in His place, empowered by the Spirit, and do even more ministry, *even greater works*, than He had done in the past three years.

It is in this context that Jesus made a bold statement, and repeated it for emphasis four times:
Whatever you ask in My name, that will I do (14:13);
Ask whatever you wish, and it will be done for you (15:7);
Whatever you ask of the Father in My name He may give to you (15:16);
If you ask the Father for anything in My name, He will give it to you (16:23).

What were Jesus' works? What did He do that His disciples (including you and me) would be able to do to an even greater extent? Every miracle He performed, every lesson taught was a sign; confirmation so that His *final work* on the cross would be **believed** by those who witnessed it. He accomplished salvation, and now the disciples would go on to tell the world about it. Their works would point to His ultimate work, and the gospel would spread throughout the world, calling men, women, boys and girls to **believe.**

Live It Out

Jesus came to save. His bold promise that we could ask anything in His name, and expect to receive it, is directly tied to our mission to share the gospel. Consider the results of these answered "ask anything" prayers:

The Father is glorified (14:13)
Much fruit is produced, which glorifies the Father (15:8,16)
Our joy is made full (16:24)

What glorifies God? It is when people believe in Christ's finished work on the cross, repent of their sins, and become part of God's kingdom.

What fills us with joy? Nothing in this world is close to the joy that is ours when we know that our loved ones are a part of God's family and will spend eternity with us in heaven. No earthly pleasure or possession compares.

Are you praying powerful prayers asking God to save?
Are you seeking His heart for the lost, and His will for the unbeliever?
Are you pleading with God to open the spiritual eyes of the people you love – even the hardest hearts that seem impossible to change?
Are you interceding for unreached people groups, millions of people you will never see on this earth, but desire to meet in heaven?

Then you are praying powerful prayers that Jesus promised to answer. He alone knows *when* and *how*, but by the authority of His own words, we can pray confidently and boldly, and carry on His work that He left us to do.

John 15:16 – *You did not choose Me but I chose you, and appointed you that you would go and bear fruit, and that your fruit would remain, so that whatever you ask of the Father in My name He may give to you.*

Pray Today

Dear Father, We believe Jesus' words, and we accept the mission that You gave us on the last night before Your crucifixion. You left heaven to give us everything, and we gladly give our lives to continue Your works. We trust Your Spirit to guide our prayers, asking what glorifies You the most, and fills us with joy. Teach us to pray bold prayers for our unbelieving friends, and expect You to answer, just as You promised. In Jesus' Name, Amen.

Day 22: Prayer Frees The Captive

Take It In

Acts 12:1-5 – *Now about that time, Herod the king laid hands on some who belonged to the church in order to mistreat them. And he had James the brother of John put to death with a sword. When he saw that it pleased the Jews, he proceeded to arrest Peter also. Now it was during the days of Unleavened Bread. When he had seized him, he put him in prison, delivering him to four squads of soldiers to guard him, intending after the Passover to bring him out before the people. So Peter was kept in the prison, but prayer for him was being made fervently by the church to God.*

Think It Through

Acts 12 tells the story of Peter's physical rescue from prison, on the night before he was destined to die at the wicked hand of Herod. It encourages us on so many levels, especially as we can clearly see God act in a supernatural way in answer to the fervent prayers of His children.

Peter fully expected to die. His close friend, James, had just been executed. Herod was filled with pleasure and pride, lauded by the Jews who were praising his actions against the believers, and he was on a murderous roll. It appears he planned to arrest the most out-spoken Christians one by one and put an end to this disruption in what he considered to be his little kingdom. God, however, had another plan!

The church was praying. Many had gathered at Mary's home to intercede for Peter, and God heard their prayers. Sixteen soldiers, heavy chains and iron gates were no match for the power of intercessory prayer, and God acted in response to those fervent prayers. Literally, he freed the captive. Peter was abruptly roused out of a sound sleep by an angel. He thought he was dreaming until he found himself standing in the city streets in the dead of night, free. Peter's immediate response was to go to the place where he knew people would be praying for him and let them know God had heard their prayers and had answered.

Live It Out

Does this happen today?
Does God still free the captive?

Yes, oh yes, He does!

Jesus Himself tells us that this was the reason He came, as He stood in the synagogue in the little town of Nazareth and read from the prophet Isaiah:

The Spirit of the Lord is upon Me, because He anointed Me to preach the gospel to the poor. He has sent Me to proclaim release to the captives, and recovery of sight to the blind, to set free those who are oppressed, to proclaim the favorable year of the Lord. (Luke 4:18-19)

You and I are held captive by our sins, chained to our broken human nature and slaves of all that is wicked until Jesus frees us. Spiritually, every person who comes to know Christ in salvation is a freed captive. We are spiritually blind until He opens our eyes. We are oppressed by Satan until He claims us for His kingdom. We are rescued, redeemed, and bought by His precious blood, freed from our spiritual captivity because somebody, somewhere prayed for us. They fervently sought God's supernatural intervention to interrupt the plans our enemy had to destroy our eternal lives.

God still answers fervent prayers, and He still frees the captive.

Are you struggling to be free from some besetting sin? Pray fervently!
Are you concerned for someone's soul who is rejecting God? Pray fervently!
Are you unsure if you know Christ personally? Pray fervently!

And God will set the captive free.

Psalm 102:18-21 – *This will be written for the generation to come, that a people yet to be created may praise the Lord. For He looked down from His holy height; from heaven the Lord gazed upon the earth, to hear the groaning of the prisoner, to set free those who were doomed to death, that men may tell of the name of the Lord in Zion and His praise in Jerusalem.*

Pray Today

Dear Father, How thankful we are that no chains can hold us when You choose to act on our behalf. You broke the chains of sin and death by Jesus' sacrifice on the cross, and now He ever lives to intercede for us. Jesus is praying fervently for us to live in the freedom for which He paid. Teach us to be prayer warriors, interceding on behalf of those who are still held captive in their sins. May we see You act in supernatural ways to free our family, our friends, and our neighbors who have not yet seen You for who You are. In Jesus' Name, Amen.

Day 23: Prayer Overcomes Temptation

Take It In

Mark 14:37-38 – *And He came and found them sleeping and said to Peter, "Simon, are you asleep? Could you not keep watch for one hour? Keep watching and praying that you may not come into temptation; the spirit is willing, but the flesh is weak."*

1 Corinthians 10:12-13 – *Therefore let him who thinks he stands take heed that he does not fall. No temptation has overtaken you but such as is common to man; and God is faithful, who will not allow you to be tempted beyond what you are able, but with the temptation will provide the way of escape also, so that you will be able to endure it.*

Think It Through

Jesus' rebuke of Peter, James and John is one we all need to hear. Effective prayer that gives us victory over temptation is found in conjunction with watchfulness. **Watch and pray.**

The word "watch" is also translated as *to keep awake,* or *to be vigilant.* It has the meaning of attentiveness and expectancy, as opposed to carelessness, slackness or indifference. Jesus uses this same word as the attitude we are to maintain regarding His return: we are to be *watchful,* so that we are not caught unaware or be ashamed when He comes (Matthew 25:13, Luke 12:37, Revelation 16:15).

Jesus told His disciples to watch and pray because He knew His enemies were coming. He did not want them to be taken by surprise. They needed to be ready; the events of the next few days would challenge their faith as never before. Likewise, we must be watchful in prayer because our enemy walks about as a roaring lion, on the prowl to challenge our faith, tempting us by his attacks on our minds and hearts.

How does prayer help us defeat temptation? Here are three thoughts.

- Prayer focuses us on others, rather than ourselves. Jesus asked Peter, James and John to pray for Him as He faced the most intense spiritual battle of His human life. Instead, they relaxed. When we are thinking more about our own needs and desires, we are more susceptible to temptation. Our failure to resist sin often comes from self-absorption.

- Prayer keeps us connected to God, and in tune with His Spirit who will guide us away from temptation. God promises to provide a way of escape, but how we will know the escape route? If we are constantly connected to God in conversation and His word, we are less likely to want to sin, and we will be quick to hear and understand Him as He whispers, *This is the way, walk in it* (Isaiah 30:21).

- Prayer reminds us of our dependence on God and keeps us humble. Paul tells us to *take heed,* so we do not fall. Pride always leads to sin, and prayer keeps us from becoming prideful as we confess our weaknesses and bring our needs to God.

Live It Out

Prayer keeps us alert. It is the practical application of being watchful, because your mind must be actively engaged to pray. As we pray, God speaks to our hearts, warning us of the temptations ahead, directing our steps to walk in holiness, reminding us of His love and desire for us. Our attention moves off ourselves and focuses on Him. All the worldly pleasures and desires that tempt us away from Him are seen for the poor imitation of life that they truly are, and we are empowered by the Holy Spirit to make the better and wiser choice.

Are you tempted? Talk to Jesus.
Have you failed? Talk to Jesus.

Pray at all times. Be alert and watchful and let God keep you from temptation.

1 Peter 5:8 – *Be of sober spirit, be on the alert. Your adversary, the devil, prowls around like a roaring lion, seeking someone to devour.*

Pray Today

Dear Father, It is at Your feet that we find victory over temptation. As we come boldly to Your throne to find help in our time of need, we realize how good and holy and precious You are. In Your presence, the temporary pleasures that steal our hearts aren't quite as attractive as we thought; in fact, we see them for the ugly and offensive things they really are. Teach us to spend time with You so that we are alert and watchful, and live victorious, holy lives that please You. In Jesus' Name, Amen.

Day 24: Prayer Fills Us With Joy

Take It In

John 16:23b-24 – *In that day you will not question Me about anything. Truly, truly, I say to you, if you ask the Father for anything in My name, He will give it to you. Until now you have asked for nothing in My name; ask and you will receive, so that your joy may be made full.*

Zephaniah 3:17 – *The Lord your God is in your midst, a victorious warrior. He will exult over you with joy, He will be quiet in His love, He will rejoice over you with shouts of joy.*

Think It Through

The last instructions Jesus gave His disciples before His arrest contain precious truths that still carry us today in His physical absence. A key thought throughout is joy. Jesus wants us to know and experience real joy; not just the comfortable happiness that comes from getting what we want, but the deep well of satisfaction and fulfillment that He described earlier as the abundant life (John 10:10). He tells us that, as we petition our Father *in His [Jesus'] name*, our joy will be made full.

Earlier we talked about what it means to ask in His name, and its direct correlation to fulfilling the mission He left us to continue. Truly this brings *us* joy. But there is another side to the joy that comes from prayer that we don't often think about, that is, that our abiding prayers bring joy to God! As our hearts unite with His heart in passionate concern and pleading for the lost, we experience what Jesus prayed for us in the Garden of Gethsemane.

His truth becomes our truth. His glory becomes our glory. His mission becomes our mission. His love becomes our love. His unity with the Father becomes our unity with Him (John 17:13-26). This unity of our hearts delights and satisfies our Father; it brings Him the great pleasure and joy that Zephaniah describes.

The Lord your God is in your midst, a victorious warrior. As we abide in Him in prayer, we experience His presence. He is *in our midst.* He is the "mighty warrior who saves."

He will exult over you with joy. He will be quiet in His love. He is cheerful and glad over us, and He is "at peace" or "rests" in His love for us. He is satisfied with us because His love has accomplished salvation; we now delight Him.

He will rejoice over you with shouts of joy. Here the word "rejoice" literally means to spin around in emotion, to dance; and those "shouts of joy" are songs. God *enjoys* our presence so much it causes Him to sing and dance.

Live It Out

Is that an uncomfortable thought for you, to imagine God singing and dancing in delight because He enjoys abiding in your presence? Perhaps this picture will help. As a grandmother of two precious toddlers, it delights my heart when my children pull into my driveway for a visit. I open my door with joy and anticipation, hardly able to wait to pull those sweet babies into my arms. I cannot stop smiling and will even dance around the room with them as I cover their little faces with my kisses.

Does God delight in us any less as He sees us enter His throne room? Set aside your preconceived ideas of who He is and simply accept this truth. As we learn to abide in His presence through prayers that unite us with His heart and His glory, we are filled with unspeakable joy, and we bring pleasure and delight to His divine heart.

Are you delighted by God? Are you filled with joy as you experience His presence in prayer? Do you realize that your Heavenly Father longs for you? Do you know that it makes His heart sing and delights Him when He sees you bow your head and come into His throne room, so much that He could dance?

Let's not disappoint our Father. Let's not make Him wait. Jesus invites us to come to the Father and be filled with joy as we unite our hearts with His in prayer for the lost. Can't you see God's smile, and hear His song of joy over you?

Isaiah 25:9 – *And it will be said in that day, "Behold, this is our God for whom we have waited that He might save us. This is the Lord for whom we have waited; let us rejoice and be glad in His salvation."*

Pray Today

Dear Father, Oh how our hearts rejoice when we are in Your presence! Like a child climbing up into his father's lap, You welcome us and delight in us, and Your pure joy spills over into our lives. Teach us to come more often, to stay longer. When our days are hard, and the world discourages us, remind us of the joy that will be found in abiding prayer. In Jesus' Name, Amen.

DAY 25: PRAYER DEFEATS THE ENEMY

Take It In

Ephesians 6:11-12,18 – *Put on the full armor of God, so that you will be able to stand firm against the schemes of the devil. For our struggle is not against flesh and blood, but against the rulers, against the powers, against the world forces of this darkness, against the spiritual forces of wickedness in the heavenly places. ... With all prayer and petition pray at all times in the Spirit, and with this in view, be on the alert with all perseverance and petition for all the saints.*

Think It Through

Living in a physical world, we often forget that there is a spiritual battle going on around us, and in us. Our physical senses, sight, sound, touch, taste and smell, are constantly bombarded by the world, and as a believer, we struggle to be sensitive to the spiritual life. Our enemy is quite good at wrapping his evil and malicious intents in attractive physical packages; he is the master of disguise. We don't even realize we are in a war.

Especially regarding salvation.

Unbelievers (those who reject the gospel) are described as snared by the devil, held captive by him to do his will (2 Timothy 2:26), with their minds blinded by the god of this world (2 Corinthians 4:4). Without God's protection, an unbeliever is fair game for our adversary, the devil, who prowls around like a roaring lion, seeking someone to devour (1 Peter 5:8). Our enemy is a schemer (2 Corinthians 2:11, Ephesians 6:11), a liar and a murderer (John 8:44), and a deceiver (Revelation 12:9). He delights in stealing away the word of God before it can penetrate the heart (Luke 8:12).

Salvation is not just a matter of convincing someone of the truth. It is a rescue operation, an assault on the enemy's territory. And we will not succeed with our physical weapons of intellect and persuasion. We need reinforcements; we need to call in the Calvary!

Consider what we're up against: *For though we walk in the flesh, we do not war according to the flesh, for the weapons of our warfare are not of the flesh, but divinely powerful for the destruction of fortresses. We are destroying speculations and every lofty thing raised up against the knowledge of God, and we are taking every thought captive to the obedience of Christ.* (2 Corinthians 10:3-5)

Fortresses are strongholds. It is what an unbeliever relies on to build his argument and reasoning; it fortifies his opinions and is the grounds from which he defends his position.

Speculations are imaginations. It is a reckoning, or reasoning, a contemplation of action based on one's conscience (a conscience which is broken by sin).

Lofty things raised up against the knowledge of God. Better translated as "high things" it refers to anything lifted up as a barrier, or anything exalted.

Live It Out

How do you destroy speculations?
How do you launch an assault on spiritual fortresses?
How do you tear down the walls raised up against the knowledge of God?

We defeat a spiritual enemy with the spiritual weapon of prayer, calling out to the only victorious One able to conquer and overcome. Prayer moves the battle out of our hands and into the spiritual world where it originates. Only God can tear down every obstacle and every resistance. His Spirit alone can pierce the hardest heart with the truth of His grace and love and mercy, and the glorious light of the knowledge and recognition of Christ.

Prayer is our weapon, not only for the salvation of our friends and neighbors and loved ones, but it is our weapon for the spiritual battles of temptation and discouragement that we face every day. Prayer defeats the enemy every single time.

Pray at all times. Pray in the Spirit. Pray with perseverance. Pray on the alert.

Lay down your weapons of reason and intellect and will. Put down your righteous anger. Set aside your strategy and give up your determination. And just pray.

Pray Today

Dear Father, Oh let us not be deceived by our own thoughts and self-will, thinking we can win a spiritual war with physical weapons. Teach us to set aside all our scheming; we don't fight like the enemy. We kneel at Your feet and trust You to do what only You can do. Remind us where the power for spiritual victory comes from and teach us to pray. In Jesus' Name, Amen.

A PRACTICAL PATH TO PRAYER
Day 26 – Day 30

First of all, I urge that entreaties and prayers,
petitions and thanksgivings,
be made on behalf of all men,
for kings and all who are in authority,
so that we may lead a tranquil and quiet life in all godliness and dignity.
This is good and acceptable in the sight of God our Savior,
who desires all men to be saved and to come to the knowledge of the truth.
For there is one God, and one mediator also between God and men,
the man Christ Jesus, who gave Himself as a ransom for all,
the testimony given at the proper time.
Therefore I want the men in every place to pray,
lifting up holy hands, without wrath and dissension.
1 Timothy 2:1-6,8

Who are you praying for?
Are your prayers centered on your own needs
or are you focusing your attention on the people around you?

We are to pray for all men – those in authority, who govern our day to day
lives, and for all those whom God desires to save.

We take an effective and practical path to prayer when we
start where we live and move outward.
Pray for your neighbors.
Pray for your city.
Pray for your country – your people.
Pray for the nations – those who speak a foreign language and have
traditions and ways you don't understand – people you will never meet.

Because God hears us and desires to answer our prayers.

DAY 26: PRAY FOR YOUR NEIGHBORHOOD

Take It In

Acts 28:30-31 –*And he stayed two full years in his own rented quarters and was welcoming all who came to him, preaching the kingdom of God and teaching concerning the Lord Jesus Christ with all openness, unhindered.*

Think It Through

How did Paul end up as a prisoner in Rome? His own people, the Jews, had him arrested and tried to have him killed for preaching the gospel. As a Roman citizen, he had appealed to Caesar, and was sent by ship as a prisoner of the state. Paul had endured storms at sea, being shipwrecked on an island for several months, and was now under house arrest until Caesar would hear his case.

By all appearances, Paul was a victim of his circumstances, held captive by events completely out of his control. He was a prisoner in his own home. But the reality was that God had sovereignly orchestrated these events to position him for a gospel ministry right in the center of the crossroads of the modern world. History indicates there were upwards of a million people living in Rome at that time. Rome was a thriving center of trade, as the phrase "all roads lead to Rome" reminds us. People came from all over the known world, literally to Paul's doorstep.

What would we have done in Paul's place? Would we have recognized the God-given opportunity to preach the gospel, teach and disciple the saints, and encourage the believers? Or would we have concluded that we had been put on the shelf, limited by the physical restraints, the mental anguish of being a prisoner, and the emotional roller-coaster of false accusations?

Would we have seen the hand of a sovereign God in the faces of our neighbors, and begun to pray that God would use us to influence the people right in front of us for the gospel?

Paul had longed to visit Rome for quite some time (Romans 1:13-15). He knew there were believers there who needed spiritual encouragement and teaching and were already suffering under persecution. He was a Roman citizen, and these were his people. But it took a prison sentence to get him there.

Live It Out

Paul gives us a glimpse into prison life in his letter to the Philippians, the epistle of *joy*. He writes, *Now I want you to know, brethren, that my circumstances have turned out for the greater progress of the gospel, so that my imprisonment in the cause of Christ has been become well known throughout the whole praetorian guard and to everyone else, and that most of the brethren, trusting in the Lord because of my imprisonment, have far more courage to speak the word of God without fear.* (Philippians 1:12-14) The people closest to Paul, those right around him, were influenced for the gospel because of his attitude, his testimony, his willingness to talk about Jesus, and his prayer life. He knew God had sovereignly planted him in Rome, confined him to a house, and he prayed consistently for the gospel to spread as a direct result.

How about you? Who lives next door to you? Down the street? Across the back fence? Do you recognize the opportunity to pray for them, asking for God to set up divine appointments with you and other believers so that the story of the gospel can reach into their homes?

Like Paul, let's ask God for our neighbors to hear the gospel *unhindered* and *with all openness.* Let's pray boldly and specifically for those right around us, and trust God to open spiritual eyes and bring salvation.

Romans 13:8 – *Owe nothing to anyone except to love one another; for he who loves his neighbor has fulfilled the law.*

Pray Today

Dear Father, How different our perspective becomes when we realize that our location, our circumstances, and our challenges are divinely appointed for the greater progress of the gospel. You have a plan to spread the gospel, and we are part of it. Teach us to look not at what hinders us, but at whom the hindrance has brought us near. Remind us not to strive too quickly to change our circumstances, but to see those circumstances through Your eyes. Give us a heavenly perspective, and the grace and strength to be used by You, so that our neighbors will see Your glory and worship You. In Jesus' Name, Amen.

Day 27: Pray For Your City

Take It In

Acts 17:16-17 – *Now while Paul was waiting for them at Athens, his spirit was being provoked within him as he was observing the city full of idols. So he was reasoning in the synagogue with the Jews and the God-fearing Gentiles, and in the market place every day with those who happened to be present.*

Think It Through

Have you ever looked around at the city where you live and felt a surge of anger at sin? Perhaps you got up one morning to read your local paper and the headline made you physically ill as your community celebrates what God declares unholy. You drive through neighborhoods that once were thriving businesses, but now are abandoned buildings, filled with trash and populated by the homeless. You are appalled by what people wear, by the language that's become acceptable, by what is now considered normal. You're frustrated with the laws, the taxes, and the endless interference of the government which only demoralizes our society. You long for the old days, and you realize it's all only going to get worse.

Paul felt that way too, for a very specific reason. As he walked through the city of Athens, he noticed that everywhere he turned, there was another statue, another idol, another place of worship dedicated to a heathen god. Historians estimate there were more than 30,000 idols in the city at that time. The Bible tells us that Paul's spirit was "provoked." This word is also translated as "stirred, greatly angered, grieved, deeply distressed, troubled, upset, disturbed, exasperated." The Greek word is *paroxynō*, from which we get our word "paroxysm," an outburst of emotion or fit of violence.

So, Paul did what he always did; he began reasoning with the people. He started in the Jewish synagogues and expanded into the city streets, talking to anyone and everyone about Jesus and His resurrection. He quickly encountered another frustrating barrier. The people were not only religious, convinced that almost everything was a god, but they were also highly intelligent philosophers, consumed by constant debate and acceptance of the next new idea. Paul finds they are so open-minded they have an altar dedicated to "an unknown god" just to cover their bases. Of course, he uses this as a bridge to explain to them the God they do not know.

Paul was not angry *at* the people. He was angry that they were blinded and consumed by idol worship and pointless arguments, missing out on the joy

68

of knowing and worshipping the God who created them. The state of the city bothered him greatly, but he knew his frustration with its condition would not accomplish anything; only a renewed knowledge of God and repentant hearts would change the situation and bring eternal life to these people who were searching diligently for what they could not find on their own.

Live It Out

How about us? When we look around at the cities where we live and see the spiritual darkness, what is our response? Do we gripe about it to our neighbors? Do we go on and on about it to our children, telling them how it *used to be*? Or do we decide to do something about it?

The most powerful weapon we have against the spiritual darkness across our cities is prayer. Instead of complaining about them or wishing we lived somewhere else, we need to pray specifically for the issues and challenges that are causing the physical and spiritual destruction. We can pray for the teachers in our schools. We can pray for the city councilmen and others in government positions. We can pray for our law enforcement. We can pray that God would remove the evil influences in our streets that are destroying our children. We can pray for the pastors and Christian business men and women who are on the front lines of the battle. We can ask God to send more laborers, people who will talk about Jesus and share the gospel, which is able to change lives. And we can be those laborers where we have influence and presence.

Perhaps you love the city where you live; maybe it's the small town where you grew up or to which you finally retired. Don't take it for granted, even if it seems to be a place of old-fashioned innocence, less culturally immoral than a big city. There are still people around you who need to hear the truth about Jesus, and there is still a spiritual darkness that burns with a desire to consume all that is good. Pray for laborers in your city, and trust God to call new believers into the kingdom, just as He did in Athens a very long time ago.

Pray Today

Dear Father, Your sovereign plans include the cities we live in just as much as the neighbors we live next to. You call us to these places of spiritual darkness to do battle, and our most effective weapon is prayer. You can redeem. You can change hearts. You can overcome evil. So, we call out to You for our cities and towns. We desire them to be places where You are honored and believed. We ask You to use us personally as an influence of righteousness, and to raise up laborers for Your harvest. In Jesus' Name, Amen.

DAY 28: PRAY FOR YOUR STATE & COUNTRY

Take It In

Romans 9:1-5 – *I am telling the truth in Christ, I am not lying, my conscience testifies with me in the Holy Spirit, that I have great sorrow and unceasing grief in my heart. For I could wish that I myself were accursed, separated from Christ for the sake of my brethren, my kinsmen according to the flesh, who are Israelites, to whom belongs the adoption as sons, and the glory and the covenants and the giving of the Law and the temple service and the promises, whose are the fathers, and from whom is the Christ according to the flesh, who is over all, God blessed forever. Amen.*

Think It Through

Paul was a unique man. He was brought up to become a rabbi, a Pharisee, a teacher of the laws of God. He called himself a Hebrew of Hebrews, circumcised on the eighth day as God had commanded, born to the tribe of Benjamin of the nation of Israel. He had been taught by Gamaliel, a respected member of the Sanhedrin. He also was a Roman citizen by birth (Acts 22:28). Paul's allegiance was to Christ, but he was also proud of his heritage, and he loved his people, the Jews.

How did Paul see his Jewish heritage? God had called him as a missionary to the Gentile nations, but his heart burned for the Jewish people, *his people.* He knew their faults and weaknesses. He loved God's Law, which was unique and special to them. He knew what it meant to "keep kosher." He spoke their language and understood their slang and the double meaning of Hebrew idioms. He knew the challenges of being Jewish in a Roman world. And just like them, he knew how it felt to spend your life looking for the Messiah, and he longed for them to understand that He had come, and His name was Jesus.

You would think that as many times as Paul had been beaten, mocked, scorned, and run out of town, that he would grow tired of his people and turn his back on them. We read that he was frustrated with their unbelief, and in Antioch literally shook the dust off his feet and told them he was called to the Gentiles (Acts 13:44-52). But he never lost his heart for them, or his desire that God would remove the spiritual blindness and allow them to see the truth. He had *great sorrow* and *unceasing grief* over their separation and *could wish himself accursed* if that would bring them to repentance.

I don't think Paul ever stopped praying for his people.

Live It Out

If you think about it, the arrangement of the twelve tribes in the nation of Israel is like our United States. We have a common heritage that binds us together as a nation, but each state has its unique personality. The camaraderie and competitiveness that was shared among Jacob's twelve sons and handed down to each generation is like the rivalry of opposing state universities, and the advertisements of "best state to live in" that compete for attention. This is true in other parts of the world as well; countries have smaller divisions (states, provinces) but belong to a larger commonality.

I am an American, but I'm also born and bred a North Carolinian. I speak the same language as the rest of my country, but I have experienced the uniqueness of growing up in the mountains of a southern state. It's my unique heritage, and there is a special place in my heart for both my state and my country. I am a product of it, and God sovereignly ordained that I would be born in this place, at this time of history, for His divine purpose.

You, too, have a heritage, and a purpose. Perhaps, like me, you still live in the same place where you grew up, and you have deep roots there. Or, maybe you weren't born where you live now; your life is a blend of many places and experiences. But the same principle applies. God has put us in a particular state or province, with a governing nation, and we have the opportunity to pray for both of them, passionately and personally. In fact, God commands it.

Does your heart ache for your people?
Do you have a desire and a longing for their salvation?

Like Paul, let's pray for the place where God has planted us, and believe Him for a great movement of the Holy Spirit in the people of our heritage.

Romans 10:1 – *Brethren, my heart's desire and my prayer to God for them is for their salvation.*

Pray Today

Dear Father, How diverse is Your creation, and we see that so clearly in the faces of the people around us. As history has unfolded, You have made of us nations and states and provinces with unique differences. You have given us common bonds that strengthen us, and experiences that color our lives and unite us to one another. Teach us to love our people, those precious ones that You desire to save, and give us a passion to pray for them. In Jesus' Name, Amen.

DAY 29: PRAY FOR THE NATIONS

Take It In

Acts 2:5-11 – *Now there were Jews living in Jerusalem, devout men from every nation under heaven. And when this sound occurred, the crowd came together, and were bewildered because each one of them was hearing them speak in his own language. They were amazed and astonished, saying, "Why, are not all these who are speaking Galileans? And how is it that we each hear them in our own language to which we were born? Parthians and Medes and Elamites, and residents of Mesopotamia, Judea and Cappadocia, Pontus and Asia, Phrygia and Pamphylia, Egypt and the districts of Libya around Cyrene, and visitors from Rome, both Jews and proselytes, Cretans and Arabs—we hear them in our own tongues speaking of the mighty deeds of God."*

Think It Through

Do you realize that God speaks all languages? I've met people who speak two or three or even four languages, which is amazing to me. I've been in foreign countries where I couldn't understand a word and had to basically play charades to communicate; when a smile was the only common language we shared. God, however, is not limited by languages: He invented them.

In the beginning, all men spoke only one language, Hebrew. According to Genesis 11:1, *the whole earth used the same language and the same words.* "Language" can refer literally to lips, and is also used to describe the bank, or edge, or shore of a river or cup. The Hebrew word for "words" is primarily translated as speech or utterance, but also used for a matter or thing done, thought, or act. The picture is that the whole earth had the same boundaries on their thoughts and words, and the actions which resulted from those thoughts and words. They were able to communicate and act in a unified way, because there were no barriers to their language.

The problem arose as man's heart was innately sinful because of the fall. Their thoughts and words turned to self-promotion, self-preservation, and self-protection. This desire to be their own god spread like wildfire and they began building a great tower for their own glory. God saw that if left to themselves, they would become a world empire, a united force for evil, and so He stepped in, confused their languages, and scattered the people (Genesis 11:1-9). After this, God turned His attention to Abraham, and began to create the nation of Israel, through which He would redeem all that separated humanity from God, in the person of His Son, Jesus.

Live It Out

The rebellion of men at the tower of Babel resulted not only in separation among people, but it placed a barrier between them and God for future generations. Like a giant speed bump that slows the spread of the gospel, the words of life cannot be heard unless they are understood. How fitting that the first presentation of the gospel after Jesus' resurrection came by the disciples miraculously being able to communicate in languages *from every nation under heaven*. God could not have been clearer: the gospel is for everyone, every tribe, every tongue, every nation.

One specific way we can pray for the nations is to ask God to empower His laborers to overcome the barriers of language. His Spirit can communicate when the words are unknown. He can raise up native translators. He can give missionaries on the field a supernatural ability to learn the heart language of the people they serve. He can communicate through dreams and visions and send His laborers to explain them at just the right time. Some of us are blessed to have His words in written form, but there are many people groups with no Bible in their language. Pray for this work, as there are many faithful men and women laboring in the field of Bible translation.

God desires to communicate with man. He commanded us to go into all the world and make disciples of all the nations (Matthew 28:19). We are blessed with understanding and access to the gospel, but there are billions who are still separated from the true knowledge of God. Pray that the Living Word, Jesus, would be proclaimed clearly to the nations.

Revelation 5:9 – *And they sang a new song, saying, "Worthy are You to take the book and break its seals; for You were slain, and purchased for God with Your blood men from every tribe and tongue and people and nation."*

Pray Today

Dear Father, We find it incredibly sad that men and women were scattered across the globe because of their rebellious hearts. We know that this was not Your desire, but sin always has consequences. How thankful we are that You speak all languages, and You desire all the nations to hear about Jesus. Remind us not to be selfish with our knowledge of You or take it for granted. Make us mighty prayer warriors on behalf of our brothers and sisters in foreign lands, who have not yet heard about You. Let our prayers burn with passion as we hold up those who are laboring in Your harvest around the world. In Jesus' Name, Amen.

Day 30: Just Pray

Take It In

Romans 12:1 – *Therefore I urge you, brethren, by the mercies of God, to present your bodies a living and holy sacrifice, acceptable to God, which is your spiritual service of worship.*

Think It Through

This admonition from Paul comes just after a lengthy lesson on the spiritual state of the Jews. They had rejected the Messiah, and so God has set them aside *for a time* and offered salvation to the Gentiles. Their hearts are hard, and their spiritual eyes are blind to the gospel. We know from other prophetic scriptures that they will go through a terrible time of tribulation before the Messiah is revealed to them, and all Jews who repent and believe will be saved. God still has a merciful heart for His chosen people. He has not abandoned them.

In the meantime, God has shown mercy on the Gentile nations (everyone who is not a Jew). Salvation has come to us, and considering the mercy that has been shown to us, Paul urges us to present our bodies to God as a living and holy sacrifice. We are to be transformed by a renewed mind (the Holy Spirit's work in us), so that we become a living example of the good, well-pleasing and perfect will of God. Our changed lives become indisputable proof that God is alive, and His word is true!

Notice the only prerequisite for this joyful and holy privilege of presenting ourselves is that we are "brethren." We are believers. We are family. We are saved. And notice also that Paul has not addressed this to those believers who are sound in mind and body and abundantly gifted with physical talents, or those who are spiritual giants, or only to those with certain spiritual gifts like teaching or preaching. This admonition is for *all* believers, and we are to present our bodies as a living sacrifice, regardless of the condition of those bodies.

Your body might be tired. It might be old. All its parts might not work correctly. You might have some replacements parts. It might not look like, or sound like, or move like you want. The world might think your body is pretty useless.

But God says, **"Present it to me."**

In fact, He says that our willingness to offer our bodies as a living and holy sacrifice is "well-pleasing" or "acceptable" to Him. God is not concerned about the condition of your body; He is looking for your heart of worship.

Live It Out

Paul goes on in Romans 12 to describe what this "living and holy sacrifice" looks like practically in our lives. We recognize that He has gifted each one of us specifically, intentionally and uniquely, and we offer those gifts back in service and love to Him, and in serving one another in the body of Christ. He describes it this way:

Not lagging behind in diligence.
Fervent in spirit.
Serving the Lord.
Rejoicing in hope.
Persevering in tribulation.
Devoted to prayer.

If you have a mind that can articulate thought, you can connect with the heart of God. You can be a vital part of His kingdom work. You can see mountains move. You can encourage the body of Christ. You can hold the rope for those who are laboring in parts of the world that you may never see. By offering your body as a living and holy sacrifice, devoted to prayer, you can change the world.

As believers, we often hear one another say, "All I can do is just pray" as if it's the final, feeble effort to accomplish what God intends. The opposite is true. Prayer is the most powerful and effective place in God's economy. It is not our job to pray about the ministry, *prayer is the ministry.* It is where our will becomes aligned with His will, and His heart becomes our heart.

God wants to use you for the kingdom. Until you take your final breath and enter heaven, He has work for you to do.

Look around you.

The world is filled with people who are lost and hurting and fearful. There are brothers and sisters who are struggling. There are children who are hungry and unloved. There are laborers who are tired and discouraged. There are fields white for harvest, but no one to go.

Could it be that your part in meeting these great needs is to call out persistently, boldly, and humbly to the only One who can fix them? To ask the Lord of the harvest to send out the laborers? To take hold of the hand of the lost with one hand, and reach up to heaven with your other hand, and stand in the gap and pray?

Is there anything more powerful and effective, than to *just pray*?

If your greatest joy is to experience the infilling grace of God overflowing from you for the good of others, then the best news in all the world is that God will do the impossible through you for the salvation of the unreached peoples.
– John Piper[1]

Pray Today

Dear Father, Oh how we long to be useful to You. You have given us faith to believe in You and set a place at Your table for us as a beloved child. You have invited us into Your kingdom, and our hearts are grateful. We naturally want to give back to You. But sometimes we are deceived by the enemy to think that we are only as useful as we feel when we compare ourselves to others. We look around at people we think are more talented, more able. We see our own weaknesses and challenging circumstances as barriers that make us unworthy and unable to serve. Help us to see ourselves as You see us. Teach us to persevere when life is hard, and press into the most powerful of all kingdom work – a life of devoted prayer. Remind us that we can be part of all that You are doing simply by spending time with You, diligently interceding for those in need. And we all need You. Give us a vision of our part in Your kingdom work and raise us up as a generation as prayer warriors for the gospel. In Jesus' Name, Amen.

[1]Piper, John. Solid Joys Daily Devotional, 10-27-18, www.desiringgod.org.

A Final Word

Our hope is that you have been blessed by this devotional and renewed in your commitment to a life of prayer. If you are a believer, go and proclaim the grace of the gospel, so that God's glory will be seen. If you are not a believer, here is how you can respond to Christ's invitation of salvation, by grace.

Believe that God created you for a relationship with Him (believe).
Genesis 1:27 – *God created man in His own image, in the image of God He created him; male and female He created them.*
Colossians 1:16c – *All things have been created through Him and for Him.*

Recognize that you are separated from God (admit).
Romans 3:23 - *For all have sinned and fall short of the glory of God.*

Be willing to turn from your sin (repent).
1 John 1:9 – *If we confess our sins, He is faithful and righteous to forgive us our sins and to cleanse us from all unrighteousness.*

Acknowledge that Jesus died on the cross and rose from the grave (accept).
Romans 10:9-10 – *That if you confess with your mouth Jesus as Lord, and believe in your heart that God raised Him from the dead, you will be saved; for with the heart a person believes, resulting in righteousness, and with the mouth he confesses, resulting in salvation.*

Invite Jesus into your heart and life through the Holy Spirit (receive).
John 1:12 – *But as many as received Him, to them He gave the right to become children of God, even to those who believe in His name.*

What To Pray
Dear Jesus, I recognize that I am separated from You because of my personal sin, and I need Your forgiveness. I believe that You died on the cross to pay the penalty for my sin. I confess my sin and ask You to forgive me. By faith, I turn from my way of life to follow You and accept Your gift of salvation by grace. I ask You to come into my life and transform me. Thank You for saving me and giving me eternal life. In Jesus' Name, Amen.

If you sincerely prayed this prayer and surrendered your life to God, you are now His child. Please share this decision with another believer and ask him or her to help you get started in how to walk in your new life in Christ. We would love to hear about your decision!

AVAILABLE RESOURCES

AroundTheCornerMinistries.org

Going Around The Corner Bible Study
ISBN: 9780692781999 / List Price: $12.99
This six-session study helps believers explore the mission field in their own neighborhood and workplace. Learn to engage others through prayer and biblical good works guided by the prompts of the Holy Spirit. Gain confidence to evangelize through sharing the complete gospel and your own story and discover how to establish and equip new believers in their faith. A simple, practical and biblical strategy for disciple-making.

Going Around The Corner Bible Study, Student Edition
ISBN: 9780999131831 / List Price: $10.99
A five-session study covering the first four chapters of the original study for high school and college students with expanded commentary and practical application, focusing on reaching their campuses, dorms, and playing fields for Christ. Students will be guided into God's Word and develop an awareness and passion for sharing the gospel.

Going Around The Corner Bible Study, Leader Guide
ISBN: 9780999131824 / List Price: $3.99
Key truths for each week, with discussion starters and thoughtful questions to help your group apply the principles in the study, plus suggested group activities and practical application steps. Adaptable for Student Edition.

40 Days of Spiritual Awareness
ISBN: 9780999131800 / List Price: $9.99
A 40-day devotional to understand who God is and how He is working in the people right around you. Each day discover truth that will increase your awareness of God, yourself, other believers, and unbelievers. Be reminded of what is important: an awareness of God's work in our world, as He redeems and saves. At the end of the journey, you will realize that you are an important part of accomplishing that work and be prepared to join Him.

Living In Light of the Manger
ISBN: 9780999131817 / List Price $9.99
If the manger only has meaning during our holiday celebrations, we've missed the point of the story. Jesus was born, so that we could be *born again*. The events of His birth and the people who welcomed Him have many lessons to teach us about the glorious gospel and how Jesus came to change our lives. Discover the purpose and power of the manger through 40 daily devotions. Perfect to share the message of the gospel with friends, co-workers and neighbors.

Grace & Glory: A 50-Day Journey In The Purpose & Plan Of God
ISBN: 9780999131848 / List Price $11.99
What do we do when we face a crisis of faith? When everything we believe is challenged, and we find our feet on a path facing insurmountable obstacles? That's when we must discover (or re-discover) God's purpose for our lives and learn to live with a mindset of His grace … grace that reveals His glory.

About The Author

Sheila Alewine came to Christ at an early age, growing up in a Baptist church in Western North Carolina. She spent a lot of time in and around church with her mom who worked as the church secretary, so marrying a full-time minister came naturally. She met her husband, Todd, while attending Liberty University in Lynchburg, VA; they married in 1985 and have spent their lives serving God together while raising two daughters.

As a young mom, Sheila fell in love with Bible study when asked to join a Precept study. Throughout the years of raising their daughters, working full-time and serving in ministry, she has loved studying and teaching in the Word. Now at this time of "empty-nest" life, she is enjoying the opportunity to try her hand at writing to encourage other believers.

Sheila and her husband reside in Hendersonville, NC, where they have established *Around The Corner Ministries* to equip and encourage followers of Christ to share the gospel where they live, work and play. They love spending time with their daughters, sons-in-law, and grandchildren.

Connect with Sheila at her blog *https://sheilaalewine.com/*.

Contact Us

If this devotional has made an impact on your life, please let us know by contacting us through our website **aroundthecornerministries.org**, by email to sheila@aroundthecornerministries.org, or through our Facebook page.

Around The Corner Ministries exists to take the gospel to every neighborhood in America. Our mission is to equip followers of Jesus to engage their neighborhoods and communities with the gospel of Jesus Christ.

Around The Corner Ministries is a partner to the local church, designed to teach and train Christ-followers how to evangelize their neighborhoods, workplaces, and communities. The goal is to grow healthy local churches filled with mature believers who are comfortable and passionate about sharing their faith. If you would like more information on how our ministry can partner with your local church, please contact us.